MORE ADVANCE PRAISE FOR
Before Buddha Was Buddha

"Rafe Martin's illuminating, thoughtful, and inspiring book reveals how the core ideas of Buddhism actually play out in the realities of our lives. This is just the book my students need to put flesh on the Buddhist bones. I recommend it enthusiastically!"

—Prof. Abigail Levin, Niagara University

"When we meet the Buddha in these stories, we meet our self in our life."

—Ron Hogen Green, Zen Center of New York City

"A most wonderful commentary on the jatakas, intimately connecting us with the rich history and heritage of the Buddha's own path. Highly recommended!"

—Taigen Henderson, Toronto Zen Center

"An excellent and most useful book!"

—Danan Henry, founding teacher of Zen Center of Denver

"A great gift—wise and down-to-earth."

—Barbara Bonner, author of *Inspiring Generosity* and *Inspiring Courage*

Before Buddha Was Buddha

Learning from the Jataka Tales

———◇———

Rafe Martin

Wisdom Publications
199 Elm Street
Somerville, MA 02144 USA
wisdompubs.org

Library of Congress Cataloging-in-Publication Data

Names: Martin, Rafe, 1946– author.
Title: Before Buddha was Buddha: learning from the Jataka tales / Rafe Martin.
Description: Somerville, MA: Wisdom Publications, 2018. | Includes bibliographical references. |
Identifiers: LCCN 2017018211 (print) | LCCN 2017034144 (ebook) | ISBN
    9781614293729 (ebook) | ISBN 1614293724 (ebook) | ISBN 9781614293545
    (pbk.: alk. paper) | ISBN 1614293546 (pbk.: alk. paper)
Subjects: LCSH: Tipiṭaka. Suttapiṭaka. Khuddakanikāya. Jātaka—
    Paraphrases, English. | Jataka stories, English.
Classification: LCC BQ1462.E5 (ebook) | LCC BQ1462.E5
    M3568 2018 (print) | DDC 294.3/82325—dc23
LC record available at https://lccn.loc.gov/2017018211

ISBN 978-1-61429-354-5   ebook ISBN 978-1-61429-372-9

21 20 19 18
4 3 2 1

Cover design by Gopa&Ted2, Inc. Interior design by Kristin Goble. Set in Adobe Garamond Pro 11/13.

Wisdom Publications' books are printed on acid-free paper and meet the guidelines for permanence and durability of the Production Guidelines for Book Longevity of the Council on Library Resources.

✿ This book was produced with environmental mindfulness. For more information, please visit wisdompubs.org/wisdom-environment.

Printed in the United States of America.

Please visit fscus.org.

To Danan Henry Roshi for his teaching
and Sunyana Graef Roshi for opportunities to teach

Embody in yourself the dedication of a boy spreading his hair on muddy ground for the Buddha to walk on.

—Zen master Dogen, referencing a jataka tale

You'll be bothered from time to time by storms, fog, snow. When you are, think of those who went through it before you and say to yourself, "What they could do, I can do."

—Antoine de Saint-Exupery

Contents

Preface: Just Like Us, the Buddha Had Difficulties

The jataka tales are ancient stories found in both the Pali Canon and Sanskrit traditions, recounting the many past lives and ongoing spiritual work of Shakyamuni Buddha on his way to his final birth as the prince Siddhartha Gautama. I have lived with and been moved as well as encouraged and inspired by the jataka tales for many years. I first encountered them well before I ever began Buddhist practice (in my case, Zen practice), back in college in the mid-1960s when I first read Joseph Campbell's *Hero with a Thousand Faces.*

Jataka tales, as well as the life of Buddha, were included in that groundbreaking book, and they touched me deeply. In 1970, when I began formal Zen practice, I already had an infant son—a daughter followed four years later—so I was on the lookout as I set out on the Buddhist path, for stories a family could grow on. I recall some odd circumstances around that time, of old books of jatakas falling off shelves (literally) into my hands. We seemed drawn to each other.

I began telling jatakas as part of my work as a storyteller and later wrote several books of jatakas as well. I find that I keep returning to them. For me, they made Zen and Buddhism human. Instead of philosophy or the austere loneliness of early meditation retreats (called *sesshin* in the Zen tradition), I found at the heart of these tales a person who tried hard and had a great aspiration to live a life of wisdom and compassion, yet simultaneously found he had a long way to go.

The Buddha became a person to me, someone with a history, someone I could take as a guide. I found this vision of commitment and unfolding depth encouraging. The tales helped me to continue my own practice despite difficulties and challenges. As a Zen teacher myself now, I lead several unique retreats each year with jatakas at their core. In these "jataka sesshin," I've discovered that these old tales, looked at from the perspective of ongoing Zen practice-realization, can offer inspiration and encouragement today. In them we find the Buddha facing issues, dealing with difficulties, making tough choices, doing his work, falling down and getting back up—nothing special or fancy, just the continuing effort of spiritual practice.

This book focuses on a selection of particular jataka tales in which the Buddha in past lives faces temptations and even struggles with self-doubt as well as other issues and shortcomings. In these tales he's not beyond life's messes—its challenges and disasters—but is down in the mix, trudging through the mud with the rest of us. The stories make it clear that any issue you or I are working on today the Buddha also, in some past life, worked on as well. Nothing we're dealing with is outside the Path.

The book's structure is simple: Each story, presented in brief, is followed by a commentary pointing to its relevance to our lives and practice-realization today. (From a Zen perspective, I see Dharma practice as a matter of practicing realization, not of doing things to *get* to something called enlightenment or realization. I'll talk more about this throughout the book.) The series of stories begins with the legend of the historic Buddha's home-leaving as the Prince Siddhartha Gautama and ends with his enlightenment beneath the bodhi tree. These two are not jatakas per se, but establish the traditional context of the spiritual path set in place by the jatakas. Finally, the appendix contains a commentary on a Zen koan connecting the Buddha's efforts in the jatakas to our lives today.

Jatakas form the legendary record of the Buddha's long and winding road to that timeless moment, twenty-six hundred years ago, of perfect and complete enlightenment (*anuttara samyak sambodhi*, in Sanskrit). They show the many lifetimes of spiritual work involved in maturing from an ordinary person to a fully awakened Buddha. In classical Buddhism, *lifetime* means the span of years from birth to death. Zen allows for it to mean the lives we live in a breath, an hour, a day, a year, and so on.

Take it as you will.

Buddhist tradition holds that the Buddha himself told all the jataka tales. His "birth stories" (which, by the way, is the essential meaning of *jataka*), quickly became popular and were sculpted, painted, carved, inscribed, written, retold, and dramatized throughout Buddhist Asia. They are held in esteem by all schools of Buddhism, including Zen. Zen masters through the centuries, like Lin-chi, Wu-men, Yüan-wu, Hakuin, and Dogen, all refer to jatakas so effortlessly we assume that their communities knew the tales well. These teachers never say they are referencing jatakas, but perhaps they didn't need to, any more than we'd need to footnote "To be or not to be" from *Hamlet*, or "May the Force be with you" from *Star Wars*. The jatakas may have had the same kind of pervasive cultural resonance.

The tales make it clear that to be like the Buddha we shouldn't imitate the finished product and just sit calmly with a half-smile on our face as our life passes by. Rather, like him, we should get up and do the work of facing up to and working with our life's challenges. Rather than emulating the serene guy on the altar—the finished "product" of all those lifetimes of effort—we learn from jatakas to be the still unknown buddhas we each already are.

A note on the linguistic conventions in the Buddhist tradition: when referring to Shakyamuni Buddha in his life prior to the one in which he awakened fully to become the Buddha, he is referred to as *the Bodhisattva* (with a capital B). A *bodhisattva* (lowercased) would be anyone on the path of awakening acting with wisdom and compassion for the sake of all. The word *buddha* is said by some to have the same root as "to bud." A buddha (lowercased) is, then, a budded being, one in whom all potential has opened fully. *The* Buddha (capitalized) refers to the historic person, born Siddhartha Gautama, who became the Awakened One.

For those interested in a bit more of the background and history of the jatakas, I recommend two of my earlier books—*The Hungry Tigress: Buddhist Myths, Legends, and Jataka Tales* and *Endless Path: Awakening within the Buddhist Imagination; Jataka Tales, Zen Practice, and Daily Life*. I also recommend *The Jatakas: Birth Stories of the Buddha* translated from the Pali by Sarah Shaw.

Finally, wherever appropriate, the Pali title and number for each jataka is included at the start of each chapter.

Now—some acknowledgments: Without the guidance in Zen practice I received from Danan Henry Roshi, this book would never have seen the light of day. His meticulous and insightful exploration of our koan curriculum was, for me, transformative. Without the encouragement to use jatakas to teach the Dharma that I received from Sunyana Graef Roshi and her communities in Vermont and Costa Rica, as well as from Taigen Henderson Roshi and his Zen community in Toronto, my investigation of jatakas would probably not have continued this far. Sunyana Roshi especially and Taigen Roshi as well, made the jatakas an important part of their communities' practice and—to be blunt—forced me each year to investigate the jatakas further so as to have material ready to share in sesshin in the form of daily teisho (Zen talks). The discussions about particular jatakas that took place over the years with these communities deepened my own understanding considerably.

However, without my own practice community, Endless Path Zendo in Rochester, New York, my experience of the jatakas would never have become so intimate. Having people to share these tales with converted me from a potentially crazed curmudgeon speaking to bare walls to someone with an apparently useful social function. Endless Path members: I am grateful—believe me!

Thanks are also due to Josh Bartok, editorial director for Wisdom Publications, for believing in this book and offering enthusiastic support. It has meant a lot.

Finally without my wife Rose's patience, interest, encouragement, wisdom, and love, none of this would have been possible.

Thanks to you all!

One

Prince Siddhartha: The Crisis of Leaving Home

Nidana-Katha, the introduction to the Pali Jataka

Approaching the age of thirty, the Prince Siddhartha Gautama decides to leave the protection of his palace and head out—for the first time, legends say—onto the streets of his city. There, over a four-day period, he dramatically encounters what are called the *four ego-devastating signs.* He sees a sick man and for the first time is appalled to discover that everyone gets sick. He sees an old man and is horrified to discover that all get old. He sees a dead man and is shocked to learn that even the most privileged die. Then he sees a truth seeker, a yogi, or perhaps a wandering hermit-monk, and realizes that there is a path leading to something more. Sheltered as he's been, he's never known these things before. After taking it all in, despite the luxuries he's been accustomed to, with great resolution he abandons his home determined to find that greater truth and bring back something of value for all—or die in the attempt.

But surely you can only come home
if you've really left home, can't you?
—Ko Un

Prior to the birth of Siddhartha (whose name means "Every Wish Fulfilled"), a sage predicted that if the child were kept from knowledge of impermanence he would become a world ruler. If not, he would renounce worldly power and become the Buddha. King Suddhodana, wanting his son Siddhartha to become that great king, did all he could to keep him from the truth. So the prince grew up knowing only happiness and pleasure. But can even the most sheltered child know *only* contentment? Does the sun always only shine? Is a toe never stubbed? Does a pet never die, a chill wind never blow? Siddhartha's father was fighting the losing battle of a man taking up arms against the sea.

When Prince Siddhartha walked out of his palace and found that everything is as impermanent as dust on the wind, he was plunged into despair. Then he rallied, determined to live with open eyes without taking refuge in trance, fantasy, cynicism, or hedonism. He could not accept any version of "when you get to heaven it will make sense to you." His driving question became: "Is there a path based on facts that leads to freedom *now*?"

With his experience of the four signs—aging, sickness, death, and a truth seeker—Siddhartha's road to world-rule was demolished. Shocked, dismayed, and then determined to find an answer, he left his home, wife, newborn son, father, foster mother, and all his luxuries and attendants. He may have felt hope as well as some sense that he was being pushed by circumstance onto the very road he'd been unconsciously seeking all along. He wasn't running away, but trying to find that Way that would benefit all, including his wife and child, like a soldier going off to fight out of necessity. His faith in what was familiar and comfortable had been

2

shattered. In a sense, he wasn't *leaving* home: stripped of everything, he no longer *had* a home.

The destined path reveals itself—and the safety and security of the old homestead are gone, gone, entirely gone. Prince Siddhartha already stood at the edge of the vast, empty ground of reality. Yet it would still take even him six more years of intensely focused practice before the truth would be clear. For now, with the overwhelming loss of all the young prince had previously known and believed, he enters the first gate of noble truth—the Gate of Anguish.

With the four signs, the solid walls that had sheltered, protected, and isolated him are smashed to rubble. He sees that there is no haven from the universal catastrophe. Illness might be prevented and aging slowed, but all must eventually swirl down the great drain of death. His sense of entitlement and safety is stripped away. No longer an onlooker, exposed and vulnerable, he finds that he's been living a dream; his attractive life, a painted corpse.

This painful stripping of childish certainties is not unique. We all know exactly how that feels. At some point we've each had our own insight into the devastation. Thinking that disillusionment is final truth, some become stuck there. Others, trying to hide from their own insight, seek distractions. Perhaps much of the gross national product is the result of a mass flight from reality, driven by repressed anxiety over the inescapable truths of sickness, aging, and death. Some seek to amass not only possessions, but power as their bulwark against the defeat that deep down we all know is heading for us with the relentless pace of the ticking clock.

Prince Siddhartha's response is something different. He does not turn and run; he does not try to repress what he knows to be true. He does not hide, attempting to build a bigger, better, even more sheltering palace. He does not become enraged, taking out his despair on others. Instead he allows himself to be emotionally naked, letting everything he'd once thought to be so drop away. Experiencing the anguish of the first noble truth, he courageously lets all he's known come to *nothing*—in itself a kind of awakening.

The question of what remains when everything we've known, clung to, or believed is taken away, lies at the core of religious practice and, while difficult, can be a turning point into greater reality. Case number twenty-seven of the *Blue Cliff Record*, a classic and quite beautiful collection of Zen koans, commentaries, and verses, presents a clue: "A monk asked Yün-men, 'How is it when the trees wither and the leaves fall?' Yün-men answered, 'Body exposed in the golden breeze.'"

Nirvana is traditionally described as cool and comfortable because the heat of delusions, false passions, and self-centered clinging—the three poisons of greed, hatred, and ignorance—have been "extinguished" (one literal meaning of *nirvana*) like a candle in the wind. When all is "gone, gone, entirely gone," as the Heart Sutra says, we find not despair or nothingness but wisdom and peace.

Manjushri, the bodhisattva of transcendent wisdom, swings a sword that cuts through duality. In his other hand is the lotus of awakening, on it the book or scroll of the Prajna Paramita's *Heart of Perfect Wisdom*. This wisdom is not added to us, not gained by us—rather, over time it is revealed as the sword of practice-realization cuts through. When all we've dualistically, self-centeredly clung to is gone, nondual wisdom is revealed. Thus, losing is gaining. The greatly thorough loss called *nirvana* is an immense relief. We touch base with this in small ways in daily meditation (*zazen* in the Zen tradition) as, breath by breath, we release the ancient, dualistic burden of me "in here" and everything else "out there."

Still, it takes courage to face into the wind of impermanence, which like the Big Bad Wolf is blowing our house down. Prince Siddhartha is well prepared, sustained and guided by his own past efforts through what Zen master Dogen termed, "countless kalpas of assiduous practice"—the incalculable eons of work shown in the jataka tales.

Though the tale of home-leaving is central to classical accounts of the Buddha's life, how possible is it that even a sheltered prince would only see illness, old age, death, and a truth seeker *for the first time* at the age of twenty-nine? How likely is it that he'd never encountered a sick person or an old one? Maybe he'd never seen a dead person, but wouldn't it be hard to avoid dead pets, work animals, and bugs? Then again, perhaps there's nothing unusual about seeing *as if* for the first time. Zen mind, beginner's mind, may now be a cliché, but consider this verse from the seventeenth-century haiku poet Teishitsu:

"Ah!" I said. "Ah!"
It was all I could say—
The cherry-flowers of Mt. Yoshino!

Indeed! I see the cherry blossoms that open each spring *as if* for the first time. Wonderful beginner's mind! When was it that we first saw sickness, old age, and death with such a mind? Perhaps the prince's response is not simply naive. Perhaps with his habitual filters removed, he saw sickness, old age, and death *as if for the first time.* A haiku by another classical poet, Shohaku, hits the same note:

A starlit night;
The sky—the size of it,
The extent of it!

To be utterly struck by what is utterly familiar can be a decisive life moment. Prince Siddhartha's mind was blown open, seeing afresh what had been hiding in plain sight. Perhaps he exclaimed with this beginner's mind, "The sick man! Ah, the pity of such a life! The old woman! Alas, for the painful ugliness of such a life."

When was it that we first wised up, got slugged between the eyes by the ordinary truth that everyone gets sick? When were we gut-punched by the realization that even our own cherished bodies would stiffen with age? When were we stunned to understand down to the ventricles of our heart that everyone, the pilot, bus driver, waiter, our partner, or child, will die and no amount of wealth or success can prevent it? How many times did we walk out of our own ordinary palace thinking ourselves well protected before *our* walls came crashing down? For Siddhartha, the privileged kid from the rich side of the tracks, it hit him at the age of twenty-nine, over an intense three- or four-day period. *Wham!* And it was done. Just like that.

The fourth sign Siddhartha saw was probably not a monk. There was no Buddhism yet. What he saw was someone on the Way who, having survived the crashing down of their own palace walls, was walking with peace, dignity, even serenity amidst the rubble. When the Bodhisattva saw that, he realized that what he'd thought was the end of his road might only be the beginning.

Typically, it's as teenagers that we first begin to sense that something is amiss out in the big, wide world we're preparing to enter. In traditional cultures puberty is a time of initiation, a time to die to childish illusions and be born as functioning adults. To live fully we must die—to all that is old, habitual, and unexamined.

Zazen is our daily practice of this. Letting go of thoughts we've identified with, letting thought sequences become porous or even transparent, is a kind of dying—to old ideas, hopes, fears, and conditioning. Momentarily letting go, we wake to what and where we are. We see the wall. "Ah, the wall." We see the floor. "Ah, the grain of the wood floor." We hear the *whoosh* of traffic, barking dogs, the groaning furnace, wind blowing, the *"Caw!"* of a crow. Ordinary things are fresh and new as if seen or heard for the first time. So begins our path through the mental fog.

We enter a sangha, a community of spiritual practice. We encounter teachers, guides, and fellow seekers. If we're lucky, we come to see what the Bodhisattva saw: not that everything is OK and we can just go home again, thank goodness, and forget the anguish, but rather, that there is a Path, one that only appears—indeed, *can* only appear—when our old house lies in ruins.

Without a model or map, that Path can be hard to find. With it—which is, in a sense, what Buddhism is (a map of the Way) we begin to walk our own version of the road. It may be a long, winding, twisting road with sheer drops and fitful starts and stops. But if we keep going, keep finding our way each time we get lost, eventually what's been lost and shattered is found. And it is whole.

Then our original home is everywhere; everywhere is home. The ancient empty house that's stood from the beginning, without walls, windows, door, roof, or floor, is unbreakable. To leave or be forced from the fragile, breakable home built of our egotistic self-involvement is a first step toward coming home to what will not collapse in ruin. What is breakable must break so that what is unbreakable may be found. As Crazy Jane says to the Bishop in Yeats's poem of that name, "Nothing is sole or whole that has not been rent." Nothing can be whole unless it is first torn, broken, shattered.

Jataka tradition insists that this wasn't the first time the Bodhisattva set out from his home as a seeker of truth: In jataka number 9, of the Pali collection of 547 jataka tales, for instance, the Bodhisattva, a long-lived king, finds a single grey hair among his black locks. Taking it as a sign of impermanence sent to him by the gods, and with 84,000 years of life yet remaining to him, he leaves his throne to his son and goes off to dedicate himself to spiritual practice.

But this time, as Siddhartha Gautama, his devastation is complete. It is ripeness, the blossoming of seeds he'd planted long ago. The four ego-devastating signs were the ringing of his own jataka-set alarm clock: *Wake up! Wake up! Time to finish the job and realize enlightenment for the benefit of all.*

At some point our palace walls, too, crumble, our locked doors swing open and, like Siddhartha, we head out into the darkness where nothing can be known in its old, limited, self-centered way. Going past the boundaries of our parents' kingdom, we head for the forests and mountains, all lesser purposes burned away. In so many ways his story is our own.

Many true paths begin with disaster: Our ship sinks. Our train gets wrecked. Our plans fail. Our hearts break. A whirlwind carries our house away leaving us naked and exposed. Or we cause enough pain to others to jolt ourselves momentarily awake. If we're lucky, like Prince Siddhartha we may get a glimpse of the Path. Maybe we meet an actual person. Maybe we see a video of the Dalai Lama. Maybe we read a book. Whatever it is, there is a shift, a turning of our life's page.

The young prince in India long ago presents the pattern. But according to the jatakas, his last home-leaving had lots of preparation. He'd already been a householder, parent, monk, layperson, merchant, soldier, artist, caravan leader, hermit, bridge builder, king, prince, acrobat, sage, child of an ogre, robber, businessman, teacher, and doctor—and that's just in the human realm. There were also his many animal lives as well as lives as nonhuman beings—as serpent-like nagas, tree spirits, devas or gods. The path of awakening is not simply about being wise. The jatakas don't shy away from showing the Buddha struggling, even making mistakes. Even for the Buddha, the Path took time to mature. His sincerity, commitment, and integrity evolved. Perseverance fueled by vows was the key.

Prince Siddhartha didn't leave home to become "spiritual." It wasn't, "I've seen impermanence. Now I'm going to get enlightened." It was a more Godot-like, "How can I go on? I must go on." But young Prince Siddhartha says more: "I will find a Way that aids not just myself, but all." Even for the Buddha, dying to the old world, being stripped of everything he'd held dear, was hard. He was human, after all. Yet in that difficulty something was waking up. In losing everything, he'd found again a road to what he'd never even consciously known he'd lost.

Avalokiteshvara, bodhisattva of compassion, is sometimes shown with eleven heads, which see all beings in their suffering, and a thousand arms. Each arm has an open eye in the palm of the hand to skillfully guide the hands to where the eyes see some being in need. Heads and eyes and hands are her response to suffering, a way of doing something about it. The Bodhisattva experiencing devastation and leaving home and Avalokiteshvara opening all those eyes and hands happen at the same time.

Heading out the door *is* opening the eyes to truth. There is impermanence. There is anguish. Not to see is to have eyes shut. The path of Dharma practice, the path of minute-by-minute sustained exertion that Zen master Dogen says is our only real refuge, begins with the first noble truth—the realization of suffering, of anguish. Discovering that its cause lies in our wrong views is the second noble truth. Realizing this, we gain the power to transform our lives and end unnecessary suffering. That's the third noble truth. Walking the Path of actual practice-realization, the eightfold path in our daily lives is the fourth truth.

This Path frees us from the cause of sorrow—our own stubbornly fixed belief in a solid ego "inside" and everything else—trees, bugs, clouds, stars, mountains, rivers, animals, and people "out there."

There are people who say they don't believe in anything. Yet if you poke them, you soon see they believe in quite a lot. They believe in the fixed reality of a forever separate, forever isolated ego-self as all they are. The Buddha, too, started out as an ordinary person, believing himself separate and alone. Yet the four signs helped him cut his attachment to that belief and transformed it into the motivation for wisdom and compassion.

But he didn't *think* his way to liberation; he wasn't a philosopher. He was a *realizer*—someone who'd had enough and decided to do the work needed to wake up. The first truth is noble not because its pain is ennobling, but because it's a first step on the journey of waking up to all the good that's even now beneath our feet.

It's where Dharma practice begins.

Two

The Banyan Deer: Hard Choices

Nigrodhamiga Jataka, No. 12

The Bodhisattva is a deer king. He, his herd, plus another herd and its king are trapped in a stockade. Every day deer are shot. Each day many deer are wounded by flying arrows, and still others are injured in the mass panic that erupts in the stockade as the shooting begins. The Bodhisattva deer comes up with a way to reduce this suffering. Each day a lottery is held, one day from one herd, one day from the other. And each day, the one losing deer goes to stand before the huntsmen, leaving the others safe. When the lot falls on a pregnant doe in the other herd, she asks her king to just let her live until her fawn is old enough to survive on its own. Then she'll go and stand before the huntsmen. She says the lottery only claims one life, not two. Narrowly and rigidly interpreting the rules, her deer king refuses to free her, saying "The law is the law. The lot fell on you. There are no exceptions." She then goes to the Banyan Deer. When he hears her tale he releases her agreeing that the lottery only claims one life at a time, not two. Then he himself goes to stand before the huntsmen in her place.

The human king, shocked at such willing sacrifice, (both deer kings had already been exempted from his hunt) asks the Banyan Deer why he is offering his life. The Bodhisattva replies that as king he cares for all his people. So he is offering himself in place of a pregnant doe whose death would have also killed her unborn fawn. These words open a new path of service for the human king. To reward the Bodhisattva deer for this teaching, he tells him that he and his herd are free and can now go live in peace. The Banyan Deer says that if he and his herd are freed, the other herd will only suffer even more. They alone will be shot and killed in the stockade. So, knowing this truth, he cannot just go and live in peace. The human king then frees the other herd, telling the Banyan Deer again, to now go and be at peace. But the Banyan Deer refuses again repeating that if he accepts the king's offer and goes now, all the other four-footed animals of the forest will be hunted even more mercilessly. The whole hunt will fall on them. So he can't go and be at peace. The king then frees the other animals, but the Banyan Deer King Bodhisattva will still not accept his own and his herd's freedom until the birds and even the fish are also freed from the king's hunt. Only then does he finally leave with his herd, now truly at peace.

---◊---

The wild deer wand'ring here and there, keeps the human soul from care.

—William Blake

We like to imagine that compassion is natural to a bodhisattva—and at a certain point it probably is. But the consequences of having a heart of compassion can be dire. Think of the bodhisattvas who risked their lives to harbor Jews in Nazi-occupied Europe. Can we fathom their integrity and courage?

In both the story of Prince Siddhartha's leaving home and the Banyan Deer, the Bodhisattva faces the first noble truth of anguish/impermanence. In each instance, rather than suppressing it or turning and fleeing from the truth, he stands his ground and then takes another step forward. As the Banyan Deer he does it in the boundary realm where our human and animal natures meet.

The Bodhisattva Deer works through attachment to his own body and mind so quickly we might miss it. But surely a decision must be made. Even for such an advanced bodhisattva, this was a milestone, perhaps something even he didn't know he would or could do until the need arose for him to do it. And then he is tested again and again. Each time he has a choice—and each time he makes the tough decision again.

The liberating work of zazen—of letting self-centeredness go—can seem like torment to our ingrained egotism. In the practice of meditation, our conditioned belief in a solid, lasting, independent self, forever separate from birds, stars, trees, mountains, clouds, bugs, and people, even those we love, is put to the test. Seeing through concepts of isolated selfhood is the work of practice-realization, a way to fulfill the bodhisattva vow to save the many beings. As Dogen says in the "Genjokoan" section of the Shobogenzo:

> To study the Way is to study the self. To study the self is to forget the self. To forget the self is to be enlightened by all things of the universe. To be enlightened by all things of the universe is to cast off the body and mind of the self as well as those of others. Even the traces of enlightenment are extinguished, and a life of traceless enlightenment goes on forever.

To free others is to free ourselves; to free ourselves is the beginning of freeing others. The Bodhisattva as a deer frees himself and others.

His insight into empty connectedness segues seamlessly into action. We, too, may discover that insight into "emptiness," rather than isolating us, opens the door to more complete participation in the world.

Yet many people still think of Buddhism as a passive, maddeningly peaceful, always smiling, navel-gazing tradition. Or if they think of Zen Buddhism in particular, they think of being "in the zone" beyond irritation and pain, at ease, unencumbered, sinking three-point baskets, running a marathon, painting a masterpiece without effort, sweat, or thought. And it's true that there are such moments—but what of actual *practice*? What of the years of exertion, aching knees, anxiety before meeting with a teacher, wrong paths taken for seemingly the best of reasons? What of failures and disappointment?

They too are part of our practice and part of our lives.

And as the jatakas show, they were there in the Buddha's life and practice as well. Looking at the jatakas, we don't see escapism or quietism. What we see is a practice of attention, the work of someone dropping self-absorption and acting with courage and compassion. Yet even for the Buddha there were times when he stood at the crossroads.

The story of the Banyan Deer is a classic recounting of such a moment. Offered the chance for personal freedom after risking his life to save a doe and unborn fawn, the deer king moves forward, step by courageous step, facing down each temptation to split and run until he's saved *all* trapped deer, all forest animals, even birds and fish. It's a mind-blowing tale, embodying the deepest vow/mind of the bodhisattva. The core of Zen and of all Mahayana Buddhist practice is this vow to save or liberate *all* beings from suffering. It is the first of the "Four Vows," or "Great Vows for All," recited by Zen practitioners at the conclusion of formal periods of zazen:

The many being are numberless;
I vow to free them all.
Greed, hatred, and ignorance rise endlessly;

I vow to abandon them all.
Dharma Gates are countless;
I vow to wake to them all.
Buddha's Way is unattainable;
I vow to embody it all.

While we usually begin working on ourselves to become free of our own suffering, in time, like the Banyan Deer, we may also come to see that we can't be free unless others are free, too. Once we catch a glimpse of the reality that we're not separate but interwoven—a single "interbeing"—something shifts. We, too, start taking responsibility, doing small things to help not just ourselves but others. So begins the path of the bodhisattva, the "wisdom being."

Zen teaches that *saving* fundamentally means helping release beings from the delusion of un-enlightenment arising from attachment to the concept of a permanent self *in here* and the "many beings" *out there*. This release must also include doing what we can to free others—human and nonhuman alike—trapped in the sufferings that arise from such dualistic thinking: social and political systems built on superiority and inferiority, riches and poverty, mine and yours, in short, the whole catastrophe that addiction to egotism—the unconscious belief in a fixed, separate, permanent, and savable self or soul—gives rise to.

But how do we release others when much of the time we're hardly able to free ourselves? Causing less harm to others by being less self-involved is the essence of the second bodhisattva vow: "Greed, anger, and ignorance, rise endlessly; I vow to abandon them." This vow is about doing the work of liberation.

Letting go of attachment to self-centeredness, we make fewer unnecessary judgments and place fewer burdens on others. We free them from the burden of carrying the weight of our projections. We release friends, family, and others from our insistence that you always be *this*, that tree always be that *thing* over there, and me, myself, and glorious "I" remain the center of it all. Being less caught up in ourselves, less bound *by* ourselves, we have more energy, space, and time to be present and of use to others. Being less "here," less self-absorbed, we are more truly *here* than ever. The chirping of birds, wind in the trees, clanging heat pipes, or morning traffic can be a symphony. The light on snow or on green leaves can be a masterwork, and a conversation with a friend as transformative as a good novel.

While this is what practice helps us eventually get to, it begins by revealing how self-involved we now are, which, in turn, becomes its own motivation to go deeper and see more truly. We don't avoid reality, but transform it through attention. Zen teachers aren't gurus, but guides, correcting us when we step off the trail, nudging us back from unseen precipices, helping release us from getting caught on thorny assumptions.

"The Banyan Deer" appears in two versions in the Pali Jataka collection. The summation above recounts the Nigrodhamiga Jataka, number twelve in the Pali collection. The differences are minor in the two instances. The core of each is that a deer offers his own life to save a doe and unborn fawn, and then goes on to save all the other animals. Compassion wins out over any impulse to save the self at the expense of others. The story brings to life the great vow to liberate all beings. Mahayana Buddhism holds that selfless compassion is our real nature, that it is the nature of mind to have or *be* such a vow. In the tale, because of the Bodhisattva's selfless efforts, all are freed. Even the king and his huntsmen stop creating their own harmful karma. (It's as if a petroleum CEO today were to suddenly wake up and say, "Stop ocean drilling! We are killing living beings!")

As illustrated in this jataka, nonhuman beings simply want to live their own lives, in their own habitats, following their own life paths. Twenty-six hundred years after this tale was first told, the possibility of fulfilling this eminently reasonable request has only become more improbable. Economic pressures and population densities are turning green forests into killing stockades. The Banyan Deer jataka can speak to us as never before. It's teaching—that no one can be free and at peace unless all are—makes absolute sense.

One implication of the "Painting of a Rice Cake" section of Dogen's Shobogenzo is that dreams; stories; art; books; movies; wooden, metal, clay, and painted Buddha figures; thoughts; and vows are food. "Only painted cakes satisfy hunger," says Dogen, turning the old adage on its head. And he playfully adds, "Without painted hunger, we never become true people."

For Dogen, jataka tales are Buddha painting a picture of Buddha with the brush and ink of "countless kalpas of assiduous practice"— that is, with the determination to continue whatever comes. The Banyan Deer's teaching of compassion, courage, and interconnection is a meal more nourishing than venison. After encountering the Banyan Deer, we, like the king, may never be the same.

Still, while the Banyan Deer saved the beings in that one kingdom, did he save all? What of beings in other kingdoms, hunted by other human kings? Oskar Schindler, the hero of *Schindler's List*, an unexpected—even to himself—bodhisattva, collapsed when the war was over tormented by the realization that he could not save more lives; could not save *all*. Can our bodhisattva vow to save all beings ever truly be accomplished?

A Buddhist legend says that the bodhisattva Avalokiteshvara tried to free all beings from suffering. One head and two hands could not come close to achieving this monumental task. It was a failure from the start. Then, out of the utmost compassion, the bodhisattva's head broke into eleven heads that could see suffering anywhere. His arms shattered into a thousand arms able to bring help in any realm. Rolling up his one thousand sleeves, the bodhisattva got back to work. The failure to fulfill that vow led to even greater compassion and skill. As Zen master Wu-men writes of another context, "The failure is wonderful indeed."

No matter how hard we practice or how long we sit, there will always be failures, difficulties, errors, and disappointments. If we think that practicing Zen, even attaining a degree of enlightenment, will make all roads smooth, drive all dark clouds away, and turn our lives into a bed of roses, we'd better think again. We're going to find ourselves disillusioned and disappointed by our own naiveté! We evolve through efforts, all partial, none complete, and so, in one sense, *all* failures. And *that's* the Way!

Power for the Way, the old teachers tell us, doesn't come from staying in the calm, peaceful place we might be able to get to (or wish to get to) in our zazen. It comes from quiet sitting, yes, but then we must get up and head out into the ordinary mix of life and actually deal with what's on our plate.

Buddhism holds that throughout the universe countless buddhas have come and gone, with at least seven past buddhas on this Earth and more to come. "And yet . . . and yet . . ."—as Issa's poignant haiku written after his young daughter's death reminds us ("This world of dew is just a world of dew—and yet . . . and yet . . .")—sadly, terribly, though buddhas have come and gone, fulfilling their vows to save all beings, numberless beings are in as much anguish as ever. The hells are still full. Turn on the news, check the Internet.

Can the vow to save all beings be literal? Is it the expression of an impossible hope? Lofty goals can help us see how far we are from where we want to be. Walking in the woods at night, a far-off light shining through the trees can show us where we need to go.

A story in poet Donald Hall's *Life Work* tells of the author's meeting Henry Moore late in the sculptor's life. Hall asked, "Now that you're eighty, can you tell me what is the secret of life?" Moore answered: "The secret of life is to have a task, something you devote your entire life to, something you bring everything to, every minute of the day for your whole life. And the most important thing is—it must be something you cannot possibly do!" Lofty goals are essential.

Once two herds of deer were trapped and marked for death. One deer said "no" to that, risking his safety and that of his herd. He didn't do it to make a point. He did it because he saw that in reality, there was no way he could be free and at peace unless all beings were also free. Animal though he was, he had realized what Thich Nhat Hanh calls "interbeing." He had the perception, not owned by any one tradition, perhaps not even by any one species, of how things are: *all beings, one body.* And he did not turn from it.

That's what's so moving about the story. "The Banyan Deer" is not just a tale of heroic compassion. It's a tale of nondual prajna wisdom. The wisdom path of the bodhisattva and the path of social justice are, it turns out, one and the same.

Three

The Naga King: The Treasure of Our Human Life

Campeyya Jataka, No. 506

The Bodhisattva, a very poor man, sees Campeyya, a king of the *nagas* (wise serpent beings), being lavishly honored by the human king for helping him win a war and secure his kingdom. Seeing all this wealth, the Bodhisattva, too, wishes to be wealthy and have a life of ease. Not long after this, he becomes ill and dies. The naga king also dies.

As the Bodhisattva has been virtuous, he's reborn as the new king of the nagas of the Campa River and has riches, power, and ready access to sensual enjoyment. But he realizes that he's made a mistake and is deeply distressed—while he's gained immense literal wealth, he realizes his goal is enlightenment, and this real treasure can only be gained as a human, not a naga. Nonetheless the nagas are so welcoming that he accepts his new position and marries the beautiful naga maiden, Sumana. But he also decides that each month he'll leave his palace on the river bottom, go back on the land in the form of a silver cobra, and fast, as well as keep vows of nonharming. With the merit of these practices he'll work toward regaining a human life. His wife, Sumana, worries and asks for a way to know if he's all right when up on the land as the human world is filled with treachery. He shows her a pool in their garden under the river, and tells her of signs she'll see in it if he's in danger. "If the water turns the color of blood," he says, "it means a snake charmer has caught me."

When he's in the form of a cobra lying coiled on an ant heap, a snake charmer captures him, causing him much physical pain in the process. But remembering his vows, the Bodhisattva/naga/cobra doesn't use his poison to kill the man. Nor will he eat the frogs he's given as food as that would mean taking life and breaking his vows.

The snake charmer makes a lot of money presenting his silver cobra and making him dance. Presented to the king, the magical dance of the serpent king is a great success. Meanwhile the Bodhisattva's naga wife, Sumana, seeing the water in the pool turn red as blood, takes human form and flies through the air, searching for him. Descending into the courtyard of the palace, she reveals that the dancing serpent is a naga lord and asks the king to free him. The king does so, and then accompanies the Bodhisattva and his wife to the river, where he's allowed to descend down to the river bottom with them. Awed by the wealth he sees there, he asks, "Why did you leave all this magnificence to lie in the dust?"

"This treasure is nothing compared to the treasure of ordinary human birth," says the Bodhisattva. "A human being can realize enlightenment, the greatest treasure in the universe." When the king leaves, laden with treasure, the excess gold falling from his carts stains the earth golden colored.

———◊———

Pure and tranquilized the skin upon you was
like gold, inlaid with precious stones. . . .
As king of the nagas you performed a wondrous deed.
—"Praise of the Buddha's Former Births"

If you think that the Bodhisattva was always perfect, never had difficulties or regrets, and never made mistakes or errors of consequence, let this story stand as your corrective. A Buddhist legend offers a striking image of what it takes to be born human: a blind turtle swims in a vast sea, surfacing only once every hundred years. A board with a hole in it floats randomly on the ocean. How long will it take before the turtle sticks its head through the hole? What are the odds? Those are the odds Buddhist tradition says we've already faced in being born human. The odds of encountering the Dharma once we are human are said to be even longer. Bear in mind that to be human might not mean just looking human. What does it mean to be an actual human being? What are our odds of becoming one? How do we do it?

The central point of the legend is clear: don't waste time, don't waste this precious human life! If we fail to do our best now, it might be a long time before our chance comes around again. The sea is boundless, the board small, and the turtle quite blind.

Yet as mysterious and full of tremendous potential as human life is, we also know it can be difficult, full of loss, disappointment, misunderstanding, malice, sorrow, grief, and injustice. Painful things happen, culminating in life-taking illness and death. Being conscious and alert, endowed with memory and anticipation, we dread the inevitable falling of that final curtain. Yet Buddhist teachings say that our human birth and its opportunity to practice realization are the greatest treasure. The Campeyya Jataka goes all out to make the point clear: it is better to be human and able to practice Dharma, even if it means living in less than ideal circumstances, than to be powerful and rich, yet unable or unmotivated to do so.

The realm of power, ease, splendor, and wealth without access to enlightened practice is symbolized by nagas. In Asia, nagas are said to live in rivers, lakes, and oceans. They have handsome male or beautiful female heads and bodies that trail off to a snake's tail. Sometimes cobra hoods— one or several—might appear above their human head. Sometimes they appear human—though when they do, you may notice a cobra hood-like aura. They can be highly sensual as well as deeply spiritual. Realizing that human beings were not yet mature enough to safely handle the complete *prajna paramita* teachings (transcendental wisdom teachings, whose core is "form is exactly emptiness; emptiness exactly form"), it is said the Buddha gave these powerful teachings to the nagas for safekeeping.

Perhaps whales and dolphins were the legendary inspiration for wise, water-living, serpent-like (in the sense of being without hands or feet) beings. Their intelligence, communication skills, and kindness— even compassion—are well documented. If whales and dolphins are the source for legends of nagas, we might see why, given their compassion and equanimity, old myths say the Buddha gave them the perfect wisdom teachings to hold until we humans had matured. Myths are not fantasy but carry more than a few grains of observed truth. And if cetaceans are nagas, then their slaughter and confinement are all the more foolish. If we kill our prajna wisdom holders or drive them mad by imprisoning them in tiny tanks, what doors to our planet's well-being might we be closing forever?

If wise, powerful, and sensual nagas enjoy life in jeweled palaces beneath rivers, lakes, and seas, how could a poverty-stricken human be better off than not just any naga, but the highest-ranking naga lord? A naga lord would have wealth, wisdom, long life, and power as well as the companionship of beautiful naga maidens. Who hasn't wished for some version of such a life? Who hasn't dreamed of beauty, wealth, comfort, and power?

The story provides its own revolutionary answer: being human offers us the opportunity to practice enlightenment, which is a better, more valuable, and greater treasure than *anything*. According to Buddhist tradition, *this* is why we have been born human—not necessarily to be Buddhists, but to undertake the *practice* of becoming authentically ourselves, awake to the living nondual presence of bugs, trees, animals, people, sun, moon, stars, mountains, rivers, earth. The story puts its challenge before us: "You can have everything you've dreamed of—treasure, ease, comfort, pleasure, and long life—but no spiritual practice, no lasting freedom from ego. Or just as you are—problems and all, difficulties and all, warts, as they say, and all—you can take up a way of liberation. Which shall it be?"

Long ago, poverty-stricken, the Bodhisattva stood at this crossroad. Wishing for something better, he chose naga riches over the pains of his all-too-ordinary human life. But once his wish was fulfilled, he discovered a fly in the expensive ointment. As a naga, even a high-ranking one, he couldn't practice what any ordinary human can—the realization of enlightenment. To do that, he'd have to be human. You don't miss your water till your well runs dry. Despite the tremendous improvement in his living circumstances, he realizes he's lost rather than gained, and resolves to do whatever's necessary to regain the ordinary human condition we now all enjoy and take for granted. The challenge the story presents is simple, yet carries its hidden "sting": The real treasure we seek is right where we are, and we can find it *if* we don't let our chance go by. But, will we? There's the rub.

Of course, there are human conditions where opportunities for practice remain not only unlikely but truly all but impossible. Famine, war, violence, and poverty can keep our treasure hidden, destroying opportunities for awakening and generating lasting harm. Working to establish a society of equality, justice, and peace—conditions that foster opportunities for awareness—is not a frill of bodhisattva work, but essential to it.

Still, isn't it natural to wish to escape from difficulty? "May all beings be happy and free of suffering" is a fundamental Buddhist aspiration. Yet one of the oldest and saddest archetypal stories is that of a person who works hard, makes sacrifices, cuts deals, maybe even commits crimes, and then, securing their prize, discovers it wasn't quite what they'd supposed it to be. Certainly there's no point in *not* going for that job, that house, or seeking to win that special person as your partner. What would be the point of *not* doing work you dream of or of *not* spending your life with a person you love? There's nothing wrong with satisfaction. Yet how easy it is when seeking a personal heaven to fall from our deepest potential.

In our poverty we are "alone and afraid in a world [we] never made" as my old Zen teacher, Roshi Philip Kapleau, former chief court reporter for the Nuremberg and Tokyo War Crimes trials, would describe it. We can seek money, power, and possessions and allow greed, hatred, and self-centeredness to cloud our minds—and in so doing make the real treasure even harder to find. Eventually at some point, like the Bodhisattva in this tale, we may think, "What have I done? I have to get back to what I'm really about." Then we, too, make sincere efforts to regain our way. Even errors, as this jataka shows, can become the foundation of deeper practice. Going astray, sometimes—if we stay alert—we see more clearly what it is we really want.

The naga realm can be seen as a way of showing what happens when we have so much that we forget our deepest goals, a warning reminding us not to get stuck in limited attainments. From a Zen perspective it could be saying, "Don't linger in shimmering emptiness. Return to the ordinary world's challenges and complexities. Here is where the work gets done."

Acknowledging our periodic descents into greed, hatred, and ignorance, practicing daily we learn to release self-centeredness. Taking up a koan, following or counting the breath, or "just fully sitting," we re-find the ancient, two-legged, human path. Then staff or steering wheel or hammer or spoon or pen or baby bottle or pots and pans in hand, we set off into the turns and twists, highs and lows of daily life, grateful for this human body and coconut-sized head so prone to self-centered error, so committed to aging and death. For impermanent as it is, this "fathom-long" body-mind remains our beyond-all-price vehicle of liberation. The Buddha told the deva Rohitassa, in a sutra of that name: "In this fathom-long body I make known the world, the origin of the world, the cessation of the world, and the way leading to the cessation of the world"—in this ordinary human body, this very one.

The impoverished Bodhisattva who'd so coveted wealth and splendor renounces them in the end, giving up attachment to external treasure to become what we are now—an ordinary human being capable of realizing the great treasure-jewel of Mind. The golden-colored earth at the conclusion is simply a storytelling way of saying, "If you don't believe the truth of this, just look at the golden-colored ground. It's proof that it's all true!"

From a Buddhist perspective, our human condition is not a realm of existential nausea, but, rather, potential freedom. Roshi Kapleau, commenting in his diary on his enlightenment as recorded in the *Three Pillars of Zen*, wrote, "Feel free as a fish swimming in an ocean of cool, clear water after being stuck in a tank of glue . . . and so grateful. . . . But mostly I am grateful for my human body, for the privilege as a human being to know this Joy, like no other."

The tale also says something about power. The naga king has the power to escape, but won't cause harm to do it. He's got poison (the full tale says he could destroy a city with a single breath), but is resolved not to strike out. How do we behave in an argument with our partner, spouse, or child? Do we cling to our entrenched views? When feeling threatened, do we overreact? Can we listen, take in what is said, and hold our poison in check? Even while making errors lifetimes ago, the Buddha found a way to model a path of peace.

Han Shan, Zen hermit on Cold Mountain, wrote (as translated by J.P. Seaton, James Sanford, Arthur Tobias):

My heart is like an autumn moon
Perfectly bright in the deep green pool
Nothing can compare with it
You tell me how it can be explained.

All similes and metaphors fall short. None can do justice to the reality of Mind—the mind that sees colors, hears sounds, thinks thoughts, understands words, eats when hungry, sleeps when tired. Zen master Eisai expressed it this way: "Because I am, heaven overhangs and earth is upheld. Because I am, the sun and the moon go round. The four seasons come in succession, all things are born, because I am, that is, because of Mind."

Moons, treasure, kings, pools, rivers, nagas all just point to where "*X* marks the spot." It remains for each of us to roll up our sleeves, dig down, and find our own long-hidden gold.

Four

The Master Musician: A Bodhisattva's Anxiety and Self-Doubt

Guttila Jataka, No. 243

The Bodhisattva, as a master musician named Guttila, accepts a younger musician named Musila as a student despite misgivings about his potential for egotism. And indeed, Musila, once fully trained, immediately seeks to supplant Guttila as the king's royal musician.

The king tells him he'll pay him half of what Master Guttila receives. But Musila protests saying, "I know all he knows. Plus, he's old and his strength is failing, while I'm reaching my peak. Hold a contest between us and you'll soon see who's the better musician." The king agrees to the competition.

The aging Bodhisattva, afraid he'll be shown up in the upcoming contest, goes off and hides in the forest. But darkness and terror of lurking animals and of nonhuman, invisible things in the forest drive him back to the city at daybreak—where he again worries about losing. So again he runs back to the forest—where terror again drives him to the city.

This happens six times.

Shakra, king of the gods, comes to him and says, "Your music is so divine it reaches all the way up into the heavens. Even we gods love to hear your playing. So, as a way of saying 'thanks,' I'll now help you. Break your strings one after the other as you play, until there are none. But even then, just play on, and I guarantee your music will be even greater than before. Plus, I'll send down many goddesses to dance when you play! It will be quite a show!"

Confidence restored, the Bodhisattva returns, enters the competition, plays, and as he plays, one by one breaks his instrument's strings—and wins handsomely. He has gone totally beyond the merely technical skill of the young challenger. Later, the Bodhisattva is taken up into the heavens for a time to entertain the goddesses there. As payment for his performance he asks the goddesses to tell him how they got into heaven. "Kind deeds," they tell him. "That's what brought us here."

He returns to Earth with a new, more mature sense of how things fit together. He sees that while music can transport him to heaven for a time, kind deeds have the power to let him live there. Living well, not just playing well, becomes the core of his new teaching, something he now offers at every performance.

———◊———

When it comes to goodness, one need not avoid competing with one's teacher.

—Confucius

Zen holds that to fulfill teaching responsibilities, one must excel or go beyond one's teacher. This has nothing to do with competitiveness or one-upmanship. These days we live in a world of Musilas forced to be out for ourselves, marketing and branding at every turn, self-promotion the name of the game. The self-centeredness this can breed can become a stumbling block on the road to genuine happiness.

There is an aspect to this jataka that is troubling: its seeming lack of fairness. The master musician Guttila, the Buddha in a past life, has a god on his side! Who's going to stand a chance against *that*?

The upstart Musila *is* out for himself, but is that so surprising? "The poison of the honeybee is the artist's jealousy," wrote William Blake back in eighteenth-century England. Every artist knows that their income depends not just on the actual quality of the work, but on its perceived reputation. You can break your heart looking into the injustice of the arts. Vincent van Gogh never sold a painting. Herman Melville never received a positive word on his masterwork *Moby-Dick*. Blake died in obscurity and poverty. Even the world of children's book publishing, which I once knew something about and which used to be noted for graciousness, has become a "bunny eat bunny" world.

It sounds funny, but it's no joke. It's rough out there.

Guttila, the Buddha in a former life, as an artist ages ago lost peace of mind and faith in himself because of his ordinary desire to be recognized and respected. The Bodhisattva is human, down in the mud with the rest of us.

When Prince Siddhartha set out from his palace seeking enlightenment, he wasn't acting. He was shocked, struck to the core by impermanence, and it hurt.

When he was the Banyan Deer, he knew the terror of the hunt down to his bones. He wasn't playing at it, giving a wink, saying, "Hey, I'm really the Bodhisattva wearing an animal mask, putting on an act to point out the Way." He's an animal in danger—which is why he can risk his life to save others. He knows their terror. In each jataka he is exactly what he appears to be—a musician, a poor man, a king, a horse, a dog, a god. At the same time he is the Bodhisattva on the Path—though he himself may not know it. He's not self-conscious, just determined to do his best and keep going. Yet in the Guttila Jataka a god—in fact, the king of all the gods—stands at the troubled Bodhisattva's side and rigs the contest in his favor. What is *that* about?

Who can explain genius? A god descends, and that's all she wrote. In the movie *Amadeus*, the pious, hardworking Salieri, tries to best Mozart. He prays and works, pushing to the limits of his talent. Yet Mozart blows him out of the water without even breaking into a sweat. It is unfair and can't be explained. On NPR's *Fresh Air*, Leonard Cohen said that he sat with Bob Dylan in the sixties in Paris after a concert and Dylan asked, "How long did it take you to write 'Hallelujah'?" Cohen answered "Two years." Then he added, "I lied. It took five." Then he asked Dylan, "How long did it take you to write, 'I and I'?" Dylan answered, "Fifteen minutes."

Two kinds of genius: one works and works at it; another opens a door in his brain and a song just walks in. Both are inexplicable. Then again, how do we form thoughts and images? Maybe we're all geniuses and just don't know it.

This 2,600-year-old jataka of two musicians has a classic ring to it. It's like some old Western in which the aging sheriff must face a young gunslinger out to make a name for himself. Or it's like Darth Vader taking up his light saber against his master Obi-Wan Kenobi. Only in this version it's not the hero's wife, sidekick, town drunk, or his own wizardly powers that save him. Instead, a god descends. Even though the master musician Guttila one far-in-the-future day will be the supremely realized, supremely confident Buddha, in this tale he can't avoid suffering, anguish, and loss of faith in himself and needs help.

The Buddha-to-be loses faith in himself? Needs help? Is afraid of losing face and income? Shouldn't a future Buddha be beyond self-doubt, the flip side of pride? As this jataka shows, he's not. He's just like us.

Buddhist tradition says that those who have attained enlightenment are no different from us. They just kept at it, even with self-doubt, shortcomings, frailties, and anxieties riding their backs. And so they discovered that issues don't need to be obstacles, but can become steppingstones on a path of wisdom. "If the fool would persist in his folly he would become wise," says our wise old man of the West, William Blake.

Or, coming at it from another perspective, Zen master Keizan says:

> You may think, "The Way of the Buddha patriarchs distinguishes individuals and capacities. We are not up to it." . . . Who among the ancients was not a body born of a mother and father? Who did not have feelings of love and affection, or thoughts of fame and fortune? However once they practiced, they practiced thoroughly.

The Bodhisattva continues not just through one lifetime, but through eons, dealing with the issues that arise, letting body and mind fall away into the Unborn over and over, opening up every nook and cranny of human character and mind—going all the way.

In this jataka the Bodhisattva finds that living wisely and acting kindly are a surer path to higher states than the transportation provided by his own talent. Even so, higher states, mental and bodily healing, as well as insights into social, political, environmental, and metaphysical realities can indeed be realized through the arts. Is there anyone who doesn't owe a debt of gratitude to a song, a painting, a symphony, a play, a movie, a novel, a story?

And yet such transports, good and freeing as they may be, don't guarantee steady going—even for their creators. Many terrific artists have had destructive lives. It is a paradox. Some artists only become real through the illusion of their art. In such moments they are *there*—full and whole—able to take us with them into the presence of our own potential. Then they step off the stage, and it's gone.

The Bodhisattva in this past-life tale got caught in his career and by the terror of seeing success stripped away. Maybe he worried, "Who will I be if I'm no longer a famous musician? Will life be worth living?" In that long ago time he had a long way to go to simply be an unencumbered human being, let alone a great bodhisattva. The story says that he was kind to his ex-musician parents, supporting them in their blind old age. Yet his center of gravity still revolved around his career. Through difficulty, he comes to see how he's stuck and eventually, by the story's end, doesn't just win, but, through meeting and hearing the stories of the goddesses who enjoy his music in heaven, becomes open to going further, his art alone no longer enough.

Being an artist doesn't discount healthy and generous living. Blake, Johann Sebastian Bach, Louis Armstrong, and Rembrandt were sterling personalities and great artists. Many Zen poets, calligraphers, and painters practiced Zen along with or as the foundation of their art. They found balance, their art expressing their practice of realization, their practice nourished by the selfless joy they found in their art. Still, the talent for being fully human resides with each of us—if we actualize it. Like all skills, it will need to be worked on, will need to be *practiced*. Being born human gives us the opportunity to practice the art of being authentic human beings. It is a lifelong Path and we can always, always go further. At the same time, it is the ordinary way we walk every day.

The great violinist Paganini, imprisoned for debt, continued to play. In time his strings broke, yet he persevered, playing with fewer and fewer strings till he was playing on only one. When freed, he electrified the house at the conclusion of his first public performance by snapping all but one string and playing on with great feeling and depth. The audience was astonished, then overwhelmed. It was as if a god had entered the hall.

So: how will you play your life's unique music on a lute not simply with one string but with no strings at all? "When your bow is broken and your last arrow spent, then shoot, shoot with your whole heart," is how a Zen verse puts it. It is only in forgetting all the strings that our music becomes truly effortless and free. Giving our all, bringing attention to each breath, each koan point, each life situation, each error, each problem, each anxiety, our life's music gets better and better.

Five

The Gardener Sage: Getting Free of Attachments

Kuddala Jataka, No. 70

The Bodhisattva, a gardener, decides to leave home to fully practice the Way when he sees his old spade lying on the ground. He picks it up, starts doing a last bit of gardening—and forgets all about leaving.

Time passes.

Again he decides to leave and commit to spiritual practice. But again, picking up his spade, he is just a gardener once more.

This happens six times.

The seventh time he thinks, "If I don't go now to accomplish what I might, I never will!" Going to the river, he tosses his spade backward over his shoulder into the water. As the spade sinks, the gardener cries out, "I have won! I have triumphed!"

A king who'd just held the day on the field of battle hears this and thinks, "There's a champion whose victory seems even greater than my own!" He leads his army to the river and finds the gardener.

He asks, "Where is the conqueror who gave that shout?" The Bodhisattva answers, "I have conquered myself. What external victories can compare?"

Rising cross-legged in the air, he teaches the king, inspiring him to also practice the Way. Seeing this the king's soldiers throw down their weapons and join the Bodhisattva and the king setting out together for the mountains and a life of spiritual practice. The people of the city soon also join them.

————◊————

Cherry blossoms
Scatter at the peak of their beauty—
It is much harder for us
To fall away from our own
Attachment to the world

— Rengetsu

Everyone has shallow broken places where work needs to be done and where we struggle. This struggle with our shortcomings is central to our humanity. It is along fault lines that we may find our best route to inner transformation.

Zen sesshin can put us in touch with difficult areas, giving us a chance to work where we're raw and least skilled. Compulsions, attachments, repressed and unconscious zones of the psyche become accessible through these meditation retreats. It can be painful—and freeing.

Why do we cling to ideas, people, position, and things? Why are we afraid to let go? The Buddha also knew this anxiety and had to work to be free. Trying, failing, trying again—in time the wandering, indecisive mind of samsara becomes the committed and decisive mind of practice-realization.

It's worth noting that the Buddha didn't just sit around talking about his past lives. He only told jatakas in response to situations that arose within his community. They were a way of helping untangle knots and open gates. The story of why he chose to tell this tale is illuminating: monks had shared food with a hungry young man who thought, "Why not join them and also eat well every day?"

That young man shaved his head, took vows, put on robes, and entered the Sangha. In time he got bored. His new life was the same every day: get up, meditate, beg, eat, listen to a talk, and meditate again. Practice without personal aspiration quickly becomes stale. The food the young man enjoyed was the same every day. Imagining the treats the world might yet offer, he left the community. But when those treats did not appear, he thought again of steady meals and, who knows, perhaps of something he couldn't yet name.

He put his robes back on and began to practice again. In time he took them off again. Back and forth he went—on with the robes, off with the robes—six times. By the seventh time even he'd had enough. Disgusted, he dug in, stopped his wandering mind—internally and externally—and attained deep realization.

The monks were astonished. How could a weak-willed, indecisive man, obsessed by an attachment to food, attain such a high degree?

The Buddha, hearing their doubts, told this jataka of a past life when he'd struggled with attachment, revealing that he, too, had had similar issues and had needed to work at becoming mature. Not seeing the reality of our wholeness, we live "small," clinging to ideas and things. Blake wrote of our isolated state of mind, "More! More! / is the cry of a mistaken soul. Less than All cannot satisfy Man."

From an absolute perspective, if we can tease absolute and relative apart, we already are the perfection we seek. At the same time we have our daily stumblings along the Path. You name it, we'll cling to it. How many years does it take to throw that damned spade away and read the love letters sent by wind and rain, moon and stars, a friend's smile, the cat's meow?

A poem of Zen master Ikkyu goes:

Every day, priests minutely examine the Dharma
And endlessly chant complicated sutras.
Before doing that, though, they should learn
How to read the love letters sent by the wind
And rain, the snow and moon.

The Buddha, too, found it hard.

As a gardener he struggled with attachment—to a shovel! Back and forth he went, getting free, then running to clasp his old shovel again. Why do we think that our own path of working with attachments will be easier? "I should be less attached" is already an attachment! The question, "Why should it be so hard?" is like asking a boulder why it should be so solid, the sky why it's so blue, the grass, so green.

Pointless.

Or maybe not. Without questions, confusions, and struggles where would we be? How would we mature? Freedom includes the freedom to question, to hold tight, and when the time comes, to let go. It is never easy, despite the freedom that Zen assures us has been ours from the start.

Yet getting rid of everything might not mean destroying anything.

Perhaps the Bodhisattva's reluctance to part with his spade was not so foolish. Without attachments where would we be? The tale seems stuck in a one-sided view. Why couldn't the gardener keep gardening and also work on himself? That's what we do: live lives, raise kids, do our jobs, and maintain a practice. Isn't emptiness form, form emptiness? Why try to separate them? Thinking, "Here's the sacred over here, and there's ordinary over there," won't do. Why couldn't his path include working in his garden? Our opportunity as lay practitioners is to live the truth of the nondual Dharma where we are, as we are.

In earlier times taking the path of practice meant literally leaving home. Layman P'ang was famous in T'ang China for dumping his wealth in the river to commit to the awakened life. He and his unusual family (wife, daughter, son—all enlightened) traveled about engaging in Dharma duels with monks and masters, supporting themselves making bamboo baskets. But even Ruth Fuller Sasaki, who translated the *Sayings of Layman P'ang*, wondered what Mrs. P'ang thought about her husband's dramatic renunciation. How'd she react when he said, "Dear, you know that money we were saving? Well, I, uh, dumped it in the river. Neat, huh?!" Why didn't he donate it to a temple, a poorhouse, or an orphanage? Did he ever regret what he'd done? When the bamboo basket business was running slow or when he saw a homeless family on the street, did he wish he had some cash to put to good use? Maybe he was a hothead, a black-or-white, all-or-nothing kind of guy. Extreme clarity can be its own blindness.

Dramatic renunciations have their place in our lives and in our practice. At such times there's no point—and no way—to hold on to what's been outgrown. We've all given away things, let go of relationships, renounced views, ideas, and positions we might have once held dear.

But letting go of mean thoughts, vengeful thoughts, forlorn self-centeredness, unhealthy addictions of body-mind, and deeply mistaken certainties is what a functioning practice is really about. Subtle, undramatic, almost invisible renunciations offer few obvious benchmarks. A Japanese Buddhist saying goes, "Better to shave the heart than shave the head." In other words, it's better to cut away our delusions, than take on the outward appearance of monk or nun. It is not that the two can't go together, but shaving the heart is accorded priority. There is no need for high drama. Little, almost unseen "letting goes" mark a path of transformation, of increasing steadiness and peacefulness. That might mean washing the extra dish, shutting off the TV, reading a good book, just sitting quietly, or going on retreat for a number of days to fully engage with the practice. The river is never far away. If it can be tossed, why not toss our old spade in? What needs to remain will remain.

Easier said than done. In this jataka we get to see the effort involved for even so towering a figure as the Bodhisattva. Letting go of attachments can't mean having *no* attachments. We're human, after all. It's more likely to mean letting go of *unnecessary* attachments in order to realize something greater. Letting go of attachment to self-centered actions, we realize greater equanimity and deeper practice. Forgoing overinvolvement in what is trivial, we commit to what brings greater happiness. Giving up inordinate attachment to our own views and desires, our conception of who and what we are and the way we think things *should* be, we can experience what we truly are and have always been. Giving up a shovel, we build a hermitage, making room to come together, sit silently, and build the practice of being ordinary human beings.

Renunciation makes us traders not destroyers. We let go of one thing to transform it into another, and sometimes what is no longer needed falls away like ripe fruit from a tree. Roshi Kapleau, an ardent vegetarian himself, counseled people by saying, "There's no need to force yourself to give up meat. At some point it will give you up." Then again, sometimes with a wrenching effort a spade is tossed and, *splash!* it's over. Done. We walk on into an unknown new life, and the many beings walk with us.

Effort is not simply necessary to accomplish an aim. Zen teaching reminds us that it is a deep expression of our nature. Without effort, the practice of innate perfection might never come alive. As translated by Sonja Arntzen, Ikkyu wrote:

For six years hunger and cold pierced his bones to the marrow.
Ascetic discipline is the mysterious teaching of the Buddhas and
    Patriarchs.
I am convinced that there is no natural Shakyamuni.

Now in the world patch-robe monks
are just rice bags.

"Rice-bag" practice means doing whatever we like, stuffing ourselves like rice bags without a thought to consequences. Even the Buddha had to work at it. As Ikkyu says, there is a genuinely aspirational path, which does not come naturally. We might resist it, but in the end such sustained *exertion*, to use Dogen's term, is our refuge.

Still, "exertion" needn't mean forced or strained. There is pain enough in accepting what is and letting go of what should be let go. While there is pain in growing and maturing, there is also triumph, fulfillment, and joy. We treasure what is hard won. The good news is that we grow through each sincere effort. Avalokiteshvara's wise heads, eyes, and thousand skillful hands emerge from her wholehearted failure. Getting back up after falling down is a true expression of the Path.

The Bodhisattva as a gardener found that in trying to free himself from a compelling attachment to his shovel and his work with it in the garden, he mapped the way of dedicated practice. Though he failed a number of times, he didn't give up, and his determination grew.

The "Gardener Sage" is an encouragement talk, a gift from our ancestor, teacher, and fellow human, Shakyamuni Buddha.

Six

King of Kings: The Limit of Desire

Mandhata Jataka, No. 258

In a past so far back it is beyond all current reckoning, the Bodhisattva was Mandhata, emperor of the world. Back then, his virtue was so great he could make jewels fall from the sky. He ruled for thousands of years, and his life seemed endless.

One day he finds that he cannot satisfy some desire. Then for the first time he discovers that here on Earth desires are not always fulfilled, whereas in higher, heavenly realms they are. "Why linger here?" he thinks.

Gathering a retinue, he rises up in the mysterious "Wheel of Empire," (perhaps a kind of miraculous flying vehicle), into heaven. Greeted by the Four Heavenly Kings, he is given rule in an un-aging human body for thousands of years. One day he cannot satisfy some desire and learns that although he is in a heaven, he is not yet in the ultimate heaven. "Why stay, then?" he thinks, and up he goes again in his miraculous Wheel of Empire, all the way to the Heaven of the Thirty-Three Gods, where he is given all he desires and where Shakra, king of the gods, shares his throne with him.

After thirty million earthly years that king god's karma is exhausted, and a new Shakra takes his place. Thirty-six such Shakras come and go. Then the Bodhisattva decides what he now desires is to rule highest heaven on his own.

With that self-centered thought he falls from heaven.

Landing in a palace garden on Earth, a now-ancient man in a robe of gold, he tells the king and nobles there that he has gone the limit of pursuing pleasures. No one has gone farther in trying to satisfy desire. He now knows that desire is endless and can never be satisfied. Dying of immense old age, he vows in future lives to work to be free of desire, no longer its slave.

———◊———

It can never be satisfied, the mind, never.
—Wallace Stevens

We tend to think of the Buddha as the paragon of goodness, wisdom, and virtue—and indeed, some schools of Buddhism emphasize his perfection. Why not? Our actual, undeluded nature, the nature of all things, living and nonliving, human and nonhuman, is vast, empty, wise, compassionate, free; beyond time and space; in a word, perfect. Shakyamuni Buddha, the Buddha of our historical time period, Buddhist tradition says, not only fully realized this, but also did the work needed to embody it fully. Jataka tales show that it took even him, determined and gifted as he was, lifetimes upon lifetimes to accomplish. They also show that while he made mistakes along the way, he matured by working with each error. Roshi Kapleau used to say that anything done sincerely is not an error but a necessary part of our journey.

Yet where do we think we are going? Zen master Hakuin Ekaku in his "Song in Praise of Zazen" says, "From the very beginning all beings are Buddha." To know this personally is the point of our journey. But what is *personally*? How do we know heat or cold, taste or sound *personally*? How do we know ourselves? "Where are we going?" is ultimately like asking, "Where is the ground?" The Buddha's smile and Zen's laughter begin here.

The Divyavadana is a Sanskrit collection of past-life stories of the Buddha and other great practitioners of his time. In it, there is a more complex version of the Mandhata Jataka in which we learn that the Buddha told it just before his *parinirvana*, or passing into nirvana or death. As one of the last jatakas he ever told, this odd little tale gains in poignancy and depth. Its very briefness marks it as appropriate to a man whose life energy is fading. Odd as it is, then, we must approach it with all seriousness. At that time the Buddha offered this final teaching (as translated by Andy Rotman):

> In a previous time, Ananda, I was filled with attachment, with hate, and with delusion, and wasn't liberated from birth, old age, sickness, death, sorrow, lamentation, suffering, grief, or despair. However, experiencing the presence of death I delivered a sermon on karma such that many hundreds of thousands of beings left behind the household life and went forth as seers would do.

He then goes on to tell the Mandhata Jataka. In the Pali version, it is not "many hundreds of thousands of beings" but only an intimate group that gathers around the dying king. However, over the 2,600 years since the jataka was first told, who knows how many have been affected enough by it to momentarily let go of self-clinging. The numbers may add up.

And what is its message? "Keep going!"—an essential instruction on whatever we may want to call the Path. As one oft-quoted saying has it: As regards the spiritual life it has been said that there are only two errors: one is not starting, the other not continuing all the way. Zen asks us to continue all the way. "The Buddha's Way is unattainable, I vow to embody it fully." This is the fourth of our Great Vows for All. "All the way" means, "no kidding." All the way means full realization of *anuttara samyak sambodhi*—perfect complete enlightenment, the enlightenment that benefits all beings. Perseverance and refinement of previous views and positions are to be expected. The jatakas reveal that it will take lifetimes.

The Bodhisattva was not a novice in going all the way. In this tale, once he's realized his mistake, he doesn't cling to regret over what turned out to be millions of years of error. Instead, he did what he needed to do, found out what he needed to find out, and went on. He didn't wallow in self-pity or beat himself up. Like a scientist whose experiment gives a clear conclusion, he got his results and went on. Like some spiritual Picasso, his Blue Period ended and he started exploring other colors. The Buddha's attitude seems to have been, "I now know from personal experience that this road doesn't lead where I want to go. Feeding desire cannot lead to contentment any more than drinking salt water can assuage thirst. I've gone the route to its end. No one can go further. It's time to move on."

In classical accounts of the Buddha's life there's a time in his quest when he practices severe asceticism. His body becomes a wreck, his mind a disaster. Near death, a bag of skin and bones wound with sinews and veins, he's reached the end of the ascetic road. Looking back to that difficult time, he says, "No one had gone further in ascetic practices. I came to the end of that road and found it did not lead to liberation."

A little-known jataka, number ninety-four in the Pali collection, says that the Bodhisattva had once been an ascetic who persisted in practices so severe they actually did kill him. As he lies dying, he has a vision of hells and realizes that tormenting the body and mind is *not* the path to enlightenment. On his deathbed he lets it *all* go and attains an insight. The last remnants of that old karma play themselves out when, as the

46

ex-prince Siddhartha Gautama, desperate for enlightenment, he takes up severe ascetic practices again. Only this time he comes to its end, ceases austerities, takes proper nourishment, and leaves that painful path forever and for good. He made a mistake, saw his error, accepted the consequences, and corrected his practice—marking the mistaken trail with a warning for those who might follow. Going all the way was and is a way of saving beings.

And this is what he does in this jataka in attempting to go, not the route of asceticism, but of hedonism. But neither hedonism's acceptance of ego's demands nor asceticism's self-denial fulfill the Middle Way. The Bodhisattva knows this personally through painfully gained experience. Like an explorer or pathfinder breaking new trail, he's simply determined to discover if a promising route leads where he wants to go—or not.

This story's view of time and space is uncanny. If millions of years passed while the Bodhisattva reigned in heaven, what kind of world did he leave? Did dinosaurs roam outside his palace walls? And what's with the "Wheel of Empire"? It sounds like a UFO. Actually, aerial cars in which devas fly from world to world are mentioned in Buddhist sutras. There's even a jataka (No. 159), in which the Bodhisattva, then a talking peacock, proves to a human king that, in a past life, he was an even greater king, by pinpointing the location of a jeweled flying machine he used to fly around in back then. He says that his flying machine will be found buried in the mud beneath the bottom of a lake, which formed over it ages ago. Dutifully they drain the lake, dig down, and find the jeweled machine exactly where the peacock says it will be. Cue in *Twilight Zone* music played on sitar, veena, and tabla.

The core of our present story is that the old trail of pleasing the self, bowing to its imperious demands and suffering because the world will not attend to our desires, has been explored to its end by our trustworthy guide, Shakyamuni Buddha. With the telling of this little jataka, perhaps his last, he puts up a clear marker for all to see: "Go no further. You can *never* satisfy desire."

As the tale shows, no matter how much meat we toss into desire's maw, no matter how we bend or twist ourselves to fit its demands, desire remains desire. Conquer one world and there's the next offering even greater possibility. Desire arises from our efforts to ease the habitual sense of being an isolated, separated, interior "self." Addiction to the drug of dualism, a primal drunkenness we fall into again and again, can't lead to contentment. Sutras say it would be like expecting a phantom created by a magician to know wholeness.

Recognizing the impossibility of satisfying self-centered desire is not the insight of any one culture or tradition. In the Grimm Brothers' tale "The Fisherman and His Wife," a poor fisherman pulls a talking flounder from the sea. The fish begs for its life and the man, moved, releases it. His wife is outraged. "It was a magic fish! Go back and tell it you deserve a reward. A nice cottage instead of this hovel will do." The man returns to a now-turgid sea. He calls and, when the flounder surfaces, makes his request. The flounder grants his wish. Now they live in a nice cottage with a garden. One day the wife says, "Tell that fish we need a mansion." The man goes to the sea where green waves are darkly tossing. The flounder says, "It's done. You live in a mansion."

You can see what's coming.

How can you live happily in a mansion if you're not the ruler of all you see? So the wife becomes queen, and they now live in a palace. But that, too, is not enough. She becomes an emperor in a palace of gold. *Phooey!* No, that, too, won't do. She becomes Pope but tires of that limited spiritual power. She sees clouds blowing, the sun shining, moon and stars glowing, trees tossing and says, "I want to be God Almighty and make clouds fly, wind blow, the sun and moon rise and set." The once-blue sea is dark and foul. The wind howls. Polluted waves slam against the rocks beneath a black, chaotic sky. Oh, but the fisherman is frightened. Though his heart hammers, he calls for the fish and makes his mad request. "Go home," says the fish, and when he returns, his wife is waiting at the gate of the broken-down hovel they had at the start.

Though the Grimm Brothers never say it, maybe the fisherman and his wife now have a chance to be happy. They've gone the full route and discovered for themselves that no matter how much you get, desire is desire, and can never be satisfied. There it is—the wisdom of the Buddha in a fairy tale.

You have to hand it to the wife in that story: she had the guts to go the route and do what we might all wish—to satisfy the mind's desire. She took the fall for us and showed where wishing leads. Where is that? Back to our own, ordinary, karma-laden lives, just as they are.

If you look, you may see Wu-men's mangy little fox, (the former head of a monastery, who, as a human being, had failed to grasp the subtle truth of cause and effect) peering through the bushes out of the second koan of *The Gateless Barrier*. As Wu-men says in his commentary to that case, "If you have the single eye of realization, you will appreciate how the former head of the monastery enjoyed 500 lives of grace as a fox." We might even come to admire the wife. She desired that the sun, moon, and stars be under her command. Did she sense something of her birthright? How, she asks, can we be content with fame or wealth when we might have the sun in the morning and the moon and starry sky at night?

In the story "The Fisherman and His Wife," contentment, peace, and happiness don't come from the wife getting her wishes fulfilled. Being the slave of desire doesn't bring happiness. Nor can happiness come from suppressing desire. That would only mean forcing desire into hiding, while at the same time *desiring* to be desireless. Their life seems to get better, but the sea only gets darker.

William Blake says, "Men are admitted into Heaven not because they have curb'd . . . their Passions or have no Passions but because they have Cultivated their Understandings." He also tells us, "The road of excess leads to the palace of wisdom."

Wise and brave words, and it looks like the Bodhisattva agrees. The Bodhisattva goes the route, marking it clearly for all who follow. Even as a member of not just the 1 percent, but the 1 percent of the 1 percent, as world emperor and then as a long-lived heavenly king, he remains open to cultivating the understanding that provides release. Following his trail, cultivating understanding, we, too, can recognize that what we thought we were is not the totality of what we are. To try to fill a delusion with things that make it happy is like trying to stuff the universe into a shoebox. Our dualistic error leads to the mess of this world where wealth tramples poverty, forests are shredded, ecosystems are destroyed, species are eliminated, and air and water are treated as commodities.

We are fortunate to have the trail markers left for us by the Bodhisattva. Who knows how long we've remained in error, desire unfulfilled, dissatisfaction, or *dukkha* in the driver's seat? (The word *dukkha*, a Sanskrit term for life's suffering, refers literally to the rubbing, grinding, groaning of a wheel not turning smoothly on its axle.) Now we can go further. The deep past is behind us as we count our breath, follow our breath, take up our koan, and wholeheartedly sit. A million million anxious years fall away. The smell of incense, the sounds of traffic, the call of birds, the *drip drip* of rain, the whoosh of wind in the trees, or the whir of a furnace or air conditioner is all there is. That's it! That's it!

Wherever we are, whatever there is, we let it enter, claim us, wipe away a million years of tears. Going all the way need not mean trudging endlessly into the future. It is here, now.

Seven

Time Is Short: Letting Go, Heading Home

Bhallatiya Jataka, No. 504

Long ago, the Bodhisattva was a king named Bhallatiya, and things were not going smoothly for him. He decides that he needs a break from the complexities of work and home. One night he quietly leaves the palace and heads off alone with a pack of hounds to go hunting in the mountains. Beneath the stars, alone with his dogs, with his campfires, weapons, and skills, he feels renewed. So he stays out there, enjoying his newfound freedom and peace.

One day he hears the sounds of two people, clearly a man and woman, sobbing. Telling his dogs to stay—so as not to frighten the two—he heads up the mountain. He is again a king, someone who knows about issues and problems and now compassionately only seeks to help. He discovers not two people, but a handsome male and beautiful female *kinnara*—delicate, half-human, half-bird beings—with their arms around each other, in tears.

He asks, "What is the cause of your anguish?"

They tell him that while they wish to always be together, never parted, one night the river rose so rapidly in a storm that they were separated by a flash flood. "I had gone to gather flowers to deck our nightly bower," sobbed the male, "and was trapped on the river's other shore." "It was impossible to cross that flood," sobbed the female. "All we could do is run along the opposite banks, calling to each other through the night, for the first time ever, sundered, kept apart. This is why we weep."

The Bodhisattva says, "I don't remember any heavy rains recently. When did this happen?"

They answer, "Six hundred and ninety-seven years ago. The pain of that night has never left us."

"How long do you live?" he asks.

"A thousand summers," they answer, "never aging or experiencing ill health until one day we just fade painlessly away, like the scent of perfume or flowers fading on the air."

Stunned, the king backs away, the hair prickling along his neck. "Seven hundred years have passed," he thinks, "and yet for one night of separation, they still weep." He gathers his hounds and weapons and heads for home. He feels like he's been gone from his palace and his people quite long enough.

————◊————

I will arise and go now, and go to Innisfree.
—W.B. Yeats

The only complete translation into English of the Pali collection, published in 1895, quaintly calls the two nonhuman beings in this jataka "fairies," evoking a kind of *Midsummer Night's Dream* atmosphere for the tale. Given their deep attachment to one another and their aversion to separation, they should more properly have been called *kinnaras* as these are the traditional characteristics ascribed to such beings. Indeed, this jataka is carved in relief at the great Buddhist monument of Borobudur and, there, the two nonhumans are clearly shown as kinnaras—half-human, half-bird.

Odd encounters with nonhuman (not simply animal) beings have been recorded through the millennia. Today we might call kinnaras "aliens" and think about flying saucers or dimensional doorways. But maybe nonhuman beings have always been around. Buddhist sutras say that nagas, garudas, kinnaras, devas, asuras are part of our planet's greater ecosystem. They say, too, that worlds are scattered like grains of sand through the universe—and that, at least, modern science easily confirms.

Another thing that is odd about this little jataka is that the Bodhisattva is a hunter. The first Buddhist precept is not to kill but to cherish all life. Ahimsa or nonharming is the foundation of Buddhist ethics. So, what's going on? Hunting is killing. Buddhism holds that all beings want to live and be happy. Even bacteria resist death. It can take increasingly powerful antibiotics to wipe out a "culture," the name with which we grace bacterial colonies. Yet in this tale the Bodhisattva is a man with weapons, hounds, and a taste for grilled meat. He has not taken vows of nonharming. Perhaps this jataka is early on in his bodhisattva career. Except for the last ten, jatakas are not arranged in any order. We only theorize a sense of progression by seeing what happens.

Like the Bodhisattva in this tale, many of us today live like kings and queens of old. Periodically we, too, feel a need to heed the call, leave complexity, renounce our piles of accumulated "stuff," and head off for the simplicity of a campsite or cabin. We want to touch the ground, reconnect with nature, and have a kind of retreat. The Bodhisattva as this hunter-king long ago, like us, was already seeking Zen's "ordinary mind."

And, indeed, out in the wild he unwinds. Stars wheel overhead at night, and a golden sun rises each morning. How ordinary! How wonderful! And then comes that sobbing.

Just then, when everything is going so well, the king, touching the ground of peace, hears sobbing. Instantly his royal skills are reawakened: *"Issues!* I know about *them!"* And off he goes to investigate.

Going up the mountain alone (his dogs might have frightened the weepers—in this we see his strength and sensitivity), he finds two delicate, nonhuman beings in anguish and, being king, capable perhaps of doing something about it, asks, "What is the cause of your suffering?" It is the question beneath all our lives: "What is the cause of this suffering?" The kinnaras answer that though they always want to be together, they were, nonetheless, separated. Mythically the kinnaras are expressing their essential identity: always lover and beloved, they never produce offspring lest that disturb their perfect affection or create separation. So, this forced separation caused by the sudden downpour and flood cuts them to the core. Creatures of extraordinary, more-than-human grace and beauty, they are devastated to have been forced apart. They have no skills with which to face what life has thrust upon them. Their delicate perfection is shattered, and they cannot get over or around it. They cannot recover.

Anguish is our experience, too, of the first noble truth that will be proclaimed by the Buddha (who *is* this king and hunter!) hundreds, if not thousands or millions of lifetimes ahead. We suffer because we, too, often feel separated from what we love, forced to be where we'd rather not. The second truth reveals that the source of our anguish is our own death grip on the concept of a separated, permanent self. Our terror starts with the knowledge that this supposedly permanent self is fading, rusting with every breath. Yet we cling to it as if it were not simply provisional but solid. This is the "human condition."

"Oh, monks," said the Buddha in the Fire Sermon, "the world is on fire with the fires of greed, hatred, and ignorance." Imagining that we are separate from bugs, stars, rivers, clouds, plants, animals, and people, we try to fulfill the needs of that separated self and so light the fires of greed, hatred, and ignorance. Confused and misled, we set ourselves an impossible, delusive task. How could we be separate when every element of every atom in our bodies has arisen from the explosion of a distant star? How could it be true, when the deepest, most fulfilling moments of our lives come, not when we cling to the belief that we're separate, but when we let it go? The sense of separation that plagues us can roll up like bamboo blinds and an undiscovered, but oh-so-familiar country be revealed. As Zen master Hakuin says in his "Song in Praise of Zazen," "The place where we stand is the pure lotus land, and this very body, the body of Buddha."

Yet as the Lotus Sutra says, in the midst of the conflagration, with our house on fire, we still sit around playing games. We may lie, cheat, and steal while persistently running toward what seems to offer comfort, despite the pain it may cause. We can blindly turn from what threatens our egotism even though it might put out the blaze and bring relief.

The second noble truth, that suffering arises from an error in understanding, adds that by releasing our hold on wrong views we can be free of our self-created suffering. The third truth affirms that the doorknob is within our grasp. The fourth says that there is a way of using body and mind, a way of living that turns the knob and opens the door.

Zen adds that opening the door doesn't increase our wisdom or compassion. Instead, it returns us to the wisdom and compassion that was there from the start. Our powers and virtues are hidden due to our own limited, delusive self-centered views.

Far in the future the hunter-king will be the Prince Siddhartha Gautama. On a day like any other he will leave his sheltering palace and step out into the streets of his city. He will be on a hunt then, too—for what he doesn't yet know. On that day he will experience anguish for he will see, as if for the first time, the terror of our daily situation. He will discover the inevitability of sickness, old age, and death and understand that no matter how we yearn for permanence, no matter what securities we pile around us, we remain as impermanent as dust on the wind. And not just us, but all we love. Parents, friends, children, pets—no one and nothing lasts. Not even the self that recognizes this, that wishes it were not so, that writes or reads these words, sagely acknowledging, "Yes, it is so."

The kinnaras' grief has opened the hunter-king to what's been missing. His hunting trip isn't going to do it. There's nothing wrong with doing what restores us. We all need time away. But we can't stay. It won't solve that thing that wakes us in the night, whether we're rested or not. The clock is ticking. Sometimes we hear it loudly, and at some point hearing it becomes motivation to go farther, see more deeply, and find out what's really going on.

The kinnaras are lovely, sensitive beings. Their tender love is admirable—and, at the same time, it is sad. Gentle, fragile, yet unchanging, and thus limited creatures, they remain stunned by their experience. Overwhelmed by the bitterness of a forced separation, innocent as lambs led to slaughter, they are stuck, unable to work with their grief and move on. Deeply attached to each other as they are, they have not yet let the greater world in. We humans, while not so pure or so innocent, are made of sterner stuff. We can digest our experiences, recover, learn, and move forward, maturing though grief and losses as we go. This is our strength.

What the Bodhisattva has seen strikes a chord. The length of the kinnaras' lifespan makes the underlying issues we all face, human or nonhuman, stand out in stark relief: Life is precious and time waits for no one. Things we do not want to happen will indeed happen. Even a long and pain-free life and the guarantee of a gentle death don't offer final escape. Time lost can never be reclaimed. We must find peace and freedom where we are as we are, or like the kinnaras, we'll be stuck in an old story, unable to fully live each new moment. The Bodhisattva's close encounter with these nonhuman beings serves as a wake-up call to him. Now he decides to head home, dig in, and do his best right where he is, no longer seeking isolation and escape. He remembers what and, perhaps, who really matters. Each ordinary moment, laden with responsibilities and complexities, has become precious to him, none of it to be wasted or missed. Once gone, not an instant or iota can be reclaimed.

The king in our story comes back down the mountain with a glimmer of *something*. Call it faith, hope, insight, resolve, strength, or prajna. Call it knowledge, kindness, generosity, or skill. Whatever you call it, however faint it might be, don't overlook it. We are changed by such moments—if we don't suppress or bury them.

Two tender, nonhumans wept bitterly over a single long-gone night of separation. Though they would live for a thousand years, even such a small separation, not a minute of which could be replaced, seemed terrible. Tender as they were, they presented the king with a truth pitiless as iron: time waits for no one.

Do not waste a minute; each is fleeting and precious. Each is your life.

They reminded the king that any life, no matter how lengthy, is fraught with unavoidable complexities that are likely to bring with them discomfort, anguish, and sorrow. How do we find our peace in the great flux?

How do we find freedom when the heat and cold of painful, difficult, unwanted experiences come our way? Given all this, how do we live our lives without endlessly yearning for what is not and what has not been? The good news is that experiencing separation can help us realize how far we are from where we truly want to be. It can itself be a way of refining and correcting a too limited view. The first noble truth is noble because it is an insight into reality. Its grave music marks our first, perhaps somewhat tentative steps along the long and winding road that leads us home.

Eight

The Monkey Bodhisattva: The Horror of "Me and Mine"

Garahita Jataka, No. 219

The Bodhisattva was a monkey, the leader of a monkey troupe. Caught by a woodsman, he's brought to the king.

The king likes his new pet and takes the monkey everywhere with him, not willing to be parted from him. In this way the Bodhisattva-monkey gets to see human life at all levels: throne room, courtroom, dining room, horseraces, theater.

Eventually the king feels remorse for the monkey's confinement and decides to set his pet free. He tells his woodsman to return the monkey to the forest where he caught him and let him go. This is done.

The monkeys, astonished to see their chief alive, ask him what happened. "After I was caught, I was taken to the king and kept by him as a pet. I dined on rich foods, slept on silken cushions, and had many toys. I saw how humans live. I wore a golden collar and chain. One day the king realized I'd been stolen from my home and released me."

The monkeys ask the Bodhisattva to tell them what life among humans was like. He refuses, saying, "It was too horrible, and I will not talk about it." But they persist and finally he agrees, saying, "People exclaim, 'Mine! Mine!' 'This gold is mine,' 'It's *my* tree. Always this mine, mine!' They have no peace. They'll even kill for the sake of this awful 'me and mine'!"

Horrified at his disclosure about human life, the monkeys abandon their cherished meeting spot forever, feeling it has now been irrevocably stained by what they've heard.

———◊———

Underfoot the mud is deep.
　　—Zen saying

It's not surprising that there are a number of jatakas in which the Buddha in a past life is a monkey.

In India monkeys are as common as crows. Twenty-six hundred years ago people certainly noticed that monkeys were a lot like us. They cared for their young and were smart, nimble, entertaining, exasperating, and emotional. Jatakas reflect a full range of these behaviors.

In some tales monkeys are foolish, pulling up plants to water the roots, thereby killing what they seek to protect. In some they are strident; in others, clever. In the most well-regarded, wisdom and compassion come to the fore. In the famous Mahakapi (Great Ape) Jataka, the Bodhisattva is a monkey king who sacrifices his life to save his people by making a bridge with his own body.

In another tale the Bodhisattva-monkey saves a man who's trapped in a pit. Freed, the man bashes his savior with a rock, meaning to cook and eat him. But he's so weak after his ordeal that the blow is merely glancing. The monkey forgives him and keeping his emotions in check, even transcending them, leads the man from the forest. The Dalai Lama told this tale in Dharamsala to a largely Tibetan audience, perhaps modeling a bodhisattvic response to China's brutality toward Tibet.

In Tibetan Buddhism there is a tradition of *terma*: Dharma treasures hidden in the earth, sky, forests, and mountains. Uncovered, they offer guidance in dark times. Perhaps jatakas are Buddha's terma, left by Shakyamuni to remind us of the equality of all life, the value of selflessness, and the intricate workings of karma, as well as to reveal the prodigious commitment and work lying behind the Buddha's smile. We, too, are encouraged to get real and do the work—not just look the part.

Jatakas tie all schools of Buddhism together. In the commentary to koan case number ninety-six of the *Blue Cliff Record*, "Chaochou's Three Turning Words," Yüan-wu imagines Hui-k'e, the Second Ancestor, standing in the snow outside Bodhidharma's cave thinking, "In the past people who sought the Way put their hair in the mud for a Buddha to walk on, broke their bones and removed the marrow to gain a verse of wisdom, leapt from cliffs to feed tigers. What about me?" These are all jataka references, and while we may not have the Buddhist background to recognize such allusions in Zen teaching, for instance, they're there.

The Garahita Jataka is very brief. While the Bodhisattva isn't shown dealing with difficulties or solidifying a virtue, the whole tale is about difficulty. He's been stolen from his home, taken from family and friends, kept from his life purpose. How does he deal with these challenges? We're left to fill it in ourselves.

It's assumed we'll recognize how hard the transition from freedom to gilded captivity has been—and we're left to imagine the details. Did he experience terror when caught? Was he depressed by enslavement? Did he try to bite? Did he tug at his golden collar, nearly strangling himself to get free? Did he resent captivity? Did he long for friends and the wild? Did he eventually enjoy the food, toys, and colors, sights, and smells of city and court? Did he appreciate the king's friendship? When and how did he come to accept what could not be changed and work with, not against, his karmic circumstances? All we know is that he held his own and somehow made the best of a bad situation.

This brief monkey jataka models the Way in the midst of life's disasters and difficulties. It invites us to consider how we work with the obstacles, setbacks, injustice, and malice that come our way. It also takes the so-called "pyramid of life," that comforting mental construction with humans at the top and all other species below, and turns it over in one vigorous *flip*. It's not pretty. It's one of the rare jatakas to show not how we see monkeys, but how we look to them.

As human beings we have the potential to wake up, drop self-centeredness, and be of benefit to all. But when we give in to childish views and linger in self-centered dreams, we create the very nightmarish conditions of life on Earth we now know all too well. The tragic consequences of "me and mine" play themselves out around us every day. "Me and mine" is not an old story. It underlies our present catastrophes, fueling environmental destruction and creating wars built on imposed inequalities of class and race. Facing the consequences of "me and mine" defines our times. And this story, so clear on an issue of dire consequence for us right now, is at least twenty-six hundred years old!

While humans and animals often talk freely in jatakas, the monkey and human kings in this tale don't. Perhaps this jataka edges toward the realism of "The Tigress," that classic jataka of the starving tigress and selfless prince who offers his own body to save her and her starving cubs. They never talk either. Instead, motivation is given and action shown. Perhaps such tales don't take place in the far distant past, but are closer to our own time. Yet any child who grows up with a pet knows that animals communicate with us, often better than we do with them.

Still, in the jatakas two-way conversations are the norm. Scientists today are hoping to reestablish real interspecies chats with primates, corvids, and cetaceans as their best shots. And elephants and octopi might be possible, too. If so, the world of the jatakas is not far off.

Zen points to this reality. In koan case number sixty-nine in the *Book of Serenity*, "Nan-ch'üan's Badger and Fox":

> Nan-ch'üan addressed his assembly and said, "All the Buddhas of past, present and future do not know *It* really is. Instead, the badger and the fox know *It* really is."

What is it they know that buddhas don't? Perhaps we should find out.

What's also odd in this jataka is that the king doesn't need prompting to do the right thing. He just sets the monkey free. There's no need for the Bodhisattva-animal to convert the human king to better behavior according to the usual jataka pattern. Instead, the king seems to have real empathy and simply frees his pet, with no more drama than a simple, "Goodbye, Monkey!"

But then comes the corker.

While humans in the tale are good, the entire human world is shown to be crazy—horrifying actually—to these so-called "lesser beings." In this story those we think of as below us on life's "pyramid" don't find us funny, wise, cute, or admirable. Rather, they see us as distressingly deluded and deeply destructive.

We know that animals can be more pure in their affections than us. Perhaps you've heard of the dog, for instance, who waited every day for years at the railway station for a master who had died and will never again get off the train. And then there's the elephant who will not eat until its dog-friend is well. (This was an actual event shown on the news a few years back, *and* it's also a jataka [No. 27]). Animals can be unbelievably courageous and selfless. Dogs will attack bears to save their "owners" and lead strangers to where a child or other dog lies hurt. They will charge through flames to save humans. Even a cat may drive off a dog to protect a child.

We honor humans who do such things, seeing in their actions the highest nobility and deepest humanity, giving them medals for selflessness and heroism. Yet since animals do these things, perhaps it is not human nature we should be honoring, but our common, animal one—or better our common-to-all-life *True* Nature. How courageous and compassionate animals are to befriend us, and how tolerant of our wrong thinking, alienation, and lack of intimacy. As "intimacy" is another word for "enlightenment," how buddha-like animals are, with hair, horns, fangs, and claws intact.

Dharma practice aims to help us peel away our delusion of alienation, to get beyond our self-centered solar system with "me and mine" as its sun. It aims to free us—and the world—from the nightmare that makes us feel like strangers, mere visitors to the planet and the universe, entitled to do to other species what we would never want done to us. Zen practice allows us to reclaim our intimacy with ourselves and with all life. It's not something we have to "get," but ours from the start—*if* we only knew it. If "me and mine" even temporarily fall away, there it is.

We begin meditation practice because we have some sense that the self-centered drama with us in the starring role and everything and everyone else off to one side is dangerously skewed. We start to sit. We experience our breath. We begin to question. In time we ask, "Where is this 'me' that assumes it owns all this and has dominion over it? What is this 'mine' made of?"

Intimacy means waking up and seeing what's been here from the start. It can be overwhelming—in a good way. Yet our seeming separation promises so much that, like addicts, we return to it again and again. But the promise it holds is always around the next bend, over the next hill, after the next pay raise, past the next award or degree, just over *there* in the future, somewhere vaguely ahead. "Jam yesterday and jam tomorrow but never jam today"—as the Queen says to Alice.

But what about today? Indeed, what about *now*? What else is there?

Even the Bodhisattva-monkey was caught. Was the trap baited with sweets that even a wise monkey couldn't resist? Did he reach into the baited trap, grab the treat, and, unwilling to let go, get trapped? "Oh monkey! Let go! Let go!" When we look at the world without practice efforts, we're like Narcissus gazing into the pond, seeing the reflection of "me and mine." The good news is that we don't have to renounce people or things, or push anything away to find freedom. Freedom is ours from the start—*if* we open our eyes and wake to it. The great Zen master Dogen, commenting on the precept of not withholding spiritual or material aid says: "From the beginning, there has been no stinginess at all. Nothing has been withheld."

But freedom doesn't mean there are no boundaries.

We're not aiming for the self-centered freedom to do what we want when we want, egotistic as we please. Zen freedom means freedom from *egotism*—worlds away from "anything goes." "Since there is no me or mine, I'll take your laptop; it belongs to no one," is wrong thinking! Buddhist precepts are clear. Self-centered interpretations of emptiness won't do! Zen practice doesn't give us anything that isn't already ours. It just helps us live in the truth of things as they are.

The consequences of failing to accord with this are not just personally tragic. Because we think and, worse, *feel* that we are the center of everything, we can't help but cause harm. Glaciers melt, species and forests die never to return, and countless beings suffer. All because of an error in the way we use our own minds.

"Me and mine" is our problem. One moment of freedom from it brings benefits not in esoteric, mystical ways, but in simple, ordinary ones.

As we intrude less into our own lives and the lives of those around us, we cause less harm and live with greater satisfaction and equanimity, wisdom, and empathy. *My* job becomes my *job*; *my* tree is freed to be my *tree*; and so on. The wisdom and compassion that are our nature have room to function. Yet though wisdom and compassion *are* our nature, the paradox is that we practice to make their realization possible.

"Me and mine" can cloud them over the way a finger can block out the light of the sun. Intimacy and realization are a *practice*, a possibility to be actualized, a choice, a step we consciously take again and again. We work at it in the meditation hall and in our lives. And while we're not in dominion on this Earth—microbes and, given their sheer numbers, insects probably hold that position—we still have so much technological and economic power that the choices we make, the things we do and do not do, affect countless other lives, both human and nonhuman, for good or ill.

Long ago, the Buddha-as-a-monkey saw the horror of "Mine! Mine!"—the disease that still plagues us. The good news is that the illness can be cured. Dharma teachings and practice are medicines. Absorbing ourselves in meditation, counting or following the breath, sitting fully aware in the "thinking not-thinking" of just sitting, focusing on a koan, as well as taking responsibility for our lives, upholding precepts, apologizing, and learning to let self-centeredness fade—all of this is medicine helping us learn to at least temporarily set "me and mine" aside.

Then our original Mind can come forward. When the waters of the old pond settle and the waves become still, when all is quiet and the pond transparent as air, you can sometimes see all the way to the bottom. What is there?

The sense of peace arising from the intimacy or nonseparation that comes as we persevere in zazen is not the end of the illness of "me and mine." But it is the beginning of the end.

Perhaps one day, if we continue, we, too, will be as wise as monkeys.

Nine

Prince Temiya: Strength to Stand Firm

Temiya Kumaro Jataka, No. 538

The Bodhisattva as the infant Prince Temiya seeing his father condemn prisoners, suddenly remembers a past life when he was a king and also punished criminals. He then recalls how, as a result, he spent eighty-four thousand years in various hells until he expiated his karma and was eventually reborn in the Heaven of the Thirty-Three Gods. There the king of the gods asked him for the good of many to be reborn back on Earth. Now that he's back, the tiny infant thinks, "When grown, I'll be king. I'll do what kings do and will fall back into hell. I must get free of all this."

A goddess living in the royal umbrella had been the Bodhisattva's mother in a past life. She tells him if he's serious, he must act as if he's useless. He tells her he will.

Then he lies still and unresponsive to all temptations, as well as to all attempts to startle him or elicit some response through fear. Whatever is done, he remains unmoving. His mother sits by his bed and begs him to respond. Both his parents fall into despair. When he's sixteen, they try sexual temptation. The prince stops breathing to keep himself from responding.

The councilors who, at his birth had happily prophesied future greatness, now advise the king he must kill the prince as his very strangeness might bring bad luck to the kingdom. As the charioteer digs a grave, the prince—after sixteen years of stillness—starts to move.

To test his strength he stands up and lifts the chariot—with one hand! Then he speaks. The charioteer is overcome to see the seemingly witless, mute, deaf, paralyzed prince so full of vigor, intelligence, and life. The king even tries to convince his son to now return and accept the throne.

The prince refuses, stating that he has no interest in such things and only seeks enlightenment. Everyone is so moved by his speech and by his determination that they follow him into the forest to also take up a spiritual life.

Two other kings think to take over the territory of Ṭemiya's kingdom. Entering the abandoned city, finding weeds and creepers growing and jewels scattered freely on the ground, they are struck by impermanence. They and their armies also join Prince Temiya at his forest hermitage.

Even animals in that forest are reborn into realms of the gods. Prince Temiya gave up a kingdom but helped many beings.

---◊---

There is no repetition, only persistence.
—William James

This tale is one of the "Ten Final Jatakas," paintings of which adorn the walls of Buddhist temples in Thailand and elsewhere. These last ten stories of the Pali Jataka, Nos. 538–547, all of noble human births, reveal the final tests faced by the Bodhisattva before his birth as Prince Siddhartha Gautama.

This jataka is a simple story, repeating one test in multiple forms until—*ta da!*—with a flourish catastrophe is averted and sorrow turns to joy.

The tale's opening is striking. A newborn child recalls past lives and decides not to repeat their errors—and sees a goddess. Do babies think about past lives and see goddesses? A Jewish legend says that children in the womb know all wisdom and truth. At birth an angel touches the newborn's upper lip with a finger (leaving an indentation), and the child forgets.

The Bodhisattva in this tale, as an infant, as a child, and as an adolescent, works incredibly hard to *avoid* the very things the rest of us work so hard to get—wealth, power, status, and the perks of success.

To support him in this effort, all he has is faith in his own insight, the advice of an umbrella goddess, and his resolve. While our determination may not be as solid as his and while we probably don't hear goddesses speaking to us, our path is, like his, also based on faith—faith that there is something beyond the intellect, senses, and body, underlying yet not separate from what we see, think, or sense; faith that the Buddha wasn't a fool or a liar when he proclaimed, "Wonder of wonders! All beings are buddhas, endowed with wisdom and virtue."

The Bodhisattva's resolve is deeply rooted. When, as ex-Prince Siddhartha Gautama, he sits under the bodhi tree and Mara's army of desires, distractions, and terrors whirls upon him, he will draw on the strength he gained in this tale. "Though my blood and flesh dry up and wither away," he proclaims, "I will not move from this spot until I have attained full enlightenment."

To show the development of such determination, the jataka must present a serious challenge. Without fearful things to face, how can there be courage? For formidable resolve, there must be formidable challenge. Being unmoved by fire, rampaging elephants, serpents, and swords, unresponsive to intense heat and startling noise (trials he's put through in the full tale), and remaining unmoved by all temptations, Temiya puts the foundations in place. The stage is being set for his great enlightenment lifetimes ahead. Through testing, the Bodhisattva is gaining power for the Way.

In case twenty-five of the *Blue Cliff Record*, we hear that once the hermit of Lotus Flower Peak held up his staff and addressed his monks, "Why didn't the old worthies remain here once they reached it?" No one could answer. So he himself said, "It has no power for the Way."

The jatakas show that to gain power for the Way the Bodhisattva must be out in life's challenges and difficulties. Being tested, he discovers what he's made of. The lotus blossoming amid flames is a Buddhist image that points to this. It is said the lotus only blossoms because of the flames—enlightenment opens because of passions, temptations, mistakes, difficulties. The difficulties provide motivation. In their midst, the Buddha becomes genuine, and a person, authentic.

Sitting in zazen and wholehearted living are a pair. A meditation hall offers practice opportunities, but as lay people we get up and head out into our lives. Life practice is where and how we gain power for the Way. The challenges of life can give us the confidence and skill we need for our practice to come alive.

Even monastics today find the world at their doorstep. Political and environmental decisions and their consequences are with us at every breath, every sip of tea. Radiation and pollution drift down from the skies and drop upon us in rain and snow. There's no longer any separate, safe place. Alternately, we can't bury ourselves in the "world," get lost in distractions, and call this "integrated practice." That's like sitting in zazen busily thinking and calling it "Zen practice." Practice is "one, two, three," just this count, just this breath, just this question, just this moment, letting whatever comes, go. The Middle Way is not a compromise, but a challenge to find balance where we are.

And yet, while triumphant, this jataka is hard to take.

The prince's parents suffered terribly, and he never gives them a sign. Why didn't he speak, relieve their anguish, and make them promise to let him go when he was old enough? Why the cold-hearted drama? Perhaps the Bodhisattva needed to establish absolute fixity of purpose, so he held firm despite an insensitivity that can make us squirm. It's impressive, but not likable.

Maybe he was too young to understand the art of negotiation. Or maybe he understood the risk. As we age, we learn to accept what might have shocked us when young. Maybe the Bodhisattva-child was already wise or experienced enough to know this and so wasn't willing to bank on even his own future decisions.

The story presents an insight into karma and character. Karma is not fixed but can change. As we "study the self," which is how Dogen describes the essence of the Buddha Way, we find it surprisingly porous. Gradually we "forget" the habitual, burdensome, separative self and gain greater freedom to choose new paths. The story also shows that change is not a given, even for a bodhisattva. The issue of sex for a sixteen-year-old is presented with some realism. The Bodhisattva *is* tempted and stops himself from breathing to keep from responding. Resisting temptation is not easy, even for the Bodhisattva in his tenth-to-last life. He was human, after all.

The story's grasp of the potentially sad consequences of power and wealth are not naive either. In vivid letters Zen master Hakuin warned the Japanese nobility that their present life of comfort and ease could easily become one of pain and difficulty if, feeling entitled, they acted callously and mistreated others. Then the good karma that had brought them high would become bad karma bringing them very low.

It's a familiar story. Wealth and entitlement overwhelm character. "I deserve it. I'm entitled. So, gimme gimme gimme!" Or duty calls and a king, trusting his experts, decides to kill his own son to protect his kingdom. What might the consequences of that have been? The infant was right—being a king and wielding power can lead to very bad karma.

The story also makes it clear that we won't just float onto the spiritual path. We must dig in, go beyond our comfort zone, and do our best. Comfort zones become prisons. At each juncture we must choose to keep going or not.

The difficulty of the Bodhisattva's choices sets the events in high contrast. The Buddha, who told this tale (and, who, as Prince Temiya lived it), shows the prince's resolve by pitting everything, including the dashed hopes of loving parents, against a child's firmest decision—a narrative device that makes the integrity and will of this child vividly clear.

There is a dark side. Innocence can be naiveté, sadly lacking in sympathy. Conversely, the world of experience while jaded, can manifest skill and compassion when facing complications. Neither innocence nor experience is complete in itself. Compromise and diplomacy are hard-won, mature skills. As the British writer G.K. Chesterton wrote, "Children are innocent and love justice, while most adults are wicked and prefer mercy."

Still, the child Temiya's innocent resolve has resonance for meditators. With each sitting, each breath, we can start anew. Manjushri Bodhisattva, patron of meditation halls, shows the way. Swinging the sword of attentive practice, old habits fall away allowing us to fully enter this moment, seeing the grain in the floor, hearing the song of the robin. Practice is never a habit, but a path of awareness we choose to embody. We can give attention to our wandering minds and their old stories, or we can give our attention to the practice, letting each count, each breath, each moment, each koan be fresh and new. As we step out of the realm of habit through daily practice, our lives become fresh and new.

It can be challenging. Who knows what will happen tomorrow? Who knows what the next breath, next ring of the phone, next news report will bring?

It remains our choice to keep at it, even though tomorrow may not bring today's expected fulfillment. Yet we know where *not* practicing will bring us. Like the child in the jataka, we'll repeat what has come before. One day Prince Siddhartha opened the door, walked out of his palace, and kept going. Eventually we leave our old home of preconceptions, ruts, and habits to come home to what's always been, what might yet be.

Without the intimacy that practice brings, our lives are easily darkened with belief in what does not exist, burdened with confusion about the nature of our own selves. Even with realization, the work of no longer investing in old habits continues. Yet this act of selling water by the river is a fraud. There is no one not already in possession of enlightened nature. Zen teaching and practice make a big deal over nothing. *Not* speaking about realization leaves us stuck. To make a case *for* enlightenment creates its own problems and anxieties causing us to ask, "Am I good enough? Will I ever realize truth? Do I have enough courage, determination, commitment, aspiration?"—and on and on.

If we keep going we find our way through—but there is no easy, well-lit road. We have to do the work, dig a hole shovelful by shovelful of dirt, walk step after step, challenge after challenge toward what might seem like very distant mountains. We count from one to ten and let *everything* go, push *nothing* away. Not clinging to anything, we see what's there, become conscious of it, then release it. We take up a koan, question it, examine it, are examined by it, become it. We face the anxiety of sitting before a teacher not knowing how to answer, not knowing what he or she may do to move things along or show our own stuckness to us. We continue through the challenges and issues of our lives. As the old teachers say, to gain power for the Way we don't cling to our practice, but actualize it in life.

In the midst of difficulties, acknowledging old patterns and where they lead or have led, we can find nourishment in the Buddha's willingness to share his own past efforts. Despite what karma brings our way we, too, can stay steady, come together, and practice. Sangha gives us a safe place to step past old patterns, actualizing what we uncover in zazen before we're back in our usual life.

We don't just repeat our practice, but persist and persevere until something we cannot yet name, that hardly moves or speaks, can stand on its own. This jataka shows that persistence not only changes us, but countless others as well.

While this might seem too good to be true, every teacher from Shakyamuni on tells us we can put our faith in it. Our practice whispers it like a goddess in an umbrella. If we doubt, that's good, too. Put it to the test! We should have the resolve to find out if what the Buddha says is true.

And if or when we discover for ourselves that it *is* true, then how deep and how far can we go, how far will we go? That's all that matters. Wherever we are now, whatever we may have gained or failed to gain, we can go further.

The Bodhisattva as the child Temiya worked hard to get what we now have—a life of practice. We don't have to renounce our life. We have books, teachers, and sanghas. We can sit, question, and let go. We can forge our renunciation in the midst of the ten thousand things—passions, temptations, challenges, joys, disappointments, objects, and events. It is a noble practice.

The Path doesn't require us to make the literal renunciation of a Temiya. Our challenge is to get to the heart of it right where we are.

Still, the archetype of Prince Temiya's renunciation rings true. We will need resolve and determination. But as the jatakas show, resolve and determination grow as we continue. Difficulties are how we get stronger, helping us open fully, like lotuses blooming in fire.

Ten

Two Cousins: Working with Karma

Citta-Sambhuta Jataka, No. 498

The Bodhisattva, now a child named Citta, and his cousin Sambhuta are born on the same day. Both are members of the Chandala caste (the lowest caste, regarded as "untouchable"). As teenagers, the two boys are beaten simply for being members of that caste. Renouncing the ways of the world that despises them, they disguise themselves as Brahmins and go off to begin spiritual practice with a teacher—a path not otherwise open to Chandalas.

In time, Citta becomes senior student. At a meal Sambhuta gets hot food stuck in his throat and cries out in the language of their caste. In this way the cousins are discovered, again beaten, and driven into the forest where they continue practicing together, grow old, and die.

Reborn as fawns, they are killed by a hunter. Reborn as osprey chicks, they are killed by a bird catcher. Reborn once more as humans, Citta is the son of the king's chaplain, and Sambhuta is the prince. They grow up as friends. Sambhuta remembers the difficulty of their former lower-caste life. Citta remembers it all—that life, as well as the lives as fawns, osprey.

Citta at sixteen enters the forest for spiritual practice and gains Realization. Sambhuta becomes king, involved in issues of ruling. After fifty years Citta feels Sambhuta might be ready to join him. Using magical power, he flies to the palace garden. Sambhuta offers Citta half his kingdom. Citta reminds the king of their pasts and how karma brought them to those painful conditions and to their present good ones. He advises the king to help his people and develop good karma. Then he recites a verse about their painful lower-caste Chandala past to inspire him: "No roof to shelter from the sky, among the dogs we lay. Our mothers nursed us as they walked, but you're a king today."

When Citta flies back to the Himalayas, Sambhuta renounces the throne and joins him.

———◊———

Does an enlightened person fall under the law of cause and effect or not?

—Zen master Wu-men

It's normal to hope that because Dharma practice is such a good thing once we begin practicing only good things will happen. It can be disappointing to discover that it just isn't so.

While it's a universal wish that good people enjoy a good life and only the wicked suffer, if we keep our eyes open we soon see that things on Earth are not quite so neatly arranged.

Buddhist teaching says that karma is subtle and complex. What we experience now might be the outcome of recent thoughts and deeds or could stem from karma so old it can't even be traced in the lines of this world. Classical Buddhism says that karma can take millions of years, even millions of kalpas to ripen and catch up with us. We are all of us, then, going to be complex mixes of so-called "good" and so-called "bad" karma.

The issue of injustice can be a stumbling block for many people, especially in theistic religions. "What's wrong with The Man Upstairs? He's not right in the head," is how my father, a Jewish WWII vet who'd flown Search and Rescue over the Himalayas (China, Burma, India) would express his considerable doubt and anger about the sad, crazy, horribly unjust things he'd seen in his life. His question goes to the root of our anguish.

In short, if the supreme deity or the universe itself is good, why a Holocaust? Why spiders, gnats, and bugs that sting and bite? Why tsunamis, earthquakes, and volcanic eruptions in which innocents suffer? Why create or allow such things? Indeed, why is there suffering and evil? Why are illness and poverty visited on good, kind people while mean, selfish, nasty folk are blessed with health and prosperity? Why is there darkness and not just beautiful, sweet, healing light?

Our own version of such questions may lead us to a path of spiritual practice. Yet, once we begin walking it, we may subtly begin to think, "*Now* everything will be all right." And it's true in the deepest sense: it is and will be. But is the scenery always rosy? Are we disappointed, angry, or disillusioned when it's not? How about when we meet obstacles, injustice, or malice? Does it strike us as *wrong*? Do we think, "But it shouldn't be like this! I'm sincerely practicing Dharma!"

Roshi Kapleau used to say, speaking about Zen practice, "In the beginning it's roses, roses, roses. Then it's thorns, thorns, thorns." His point was that as our initial excitement about finding a spiritual path fades and we get down to work, things can get tough. We begin to uncover the issues and problems underlying our own ancient difficulties. We find that spiritual practice is not an escape, but a serious commitment to doing the real work. As we practice, our determination will be tested, the depths of our commitment sounded. But isn't that what we want—a goal worthy of our efforts? One that takes everything we've got? One that demands we be real, see our fears, shortcomings, and unrealistic hopes, and still go courageously on into the unknown of *this* present moment, *this* breath and the next, *this* thought and the next arising of thought, this problem, this insight. Isn't that what it should be about?

The path of sustained exertion, as Zen master Dogen called it, encompasses lifetimes—countless births, deaths, rebirths—as the jatakas show. Given our complex mix of karma, which classical Buddhism says extends back through an endless past, painful things not easy to swallow or digest are going to happen. In this jataka the Bodhisattva who'd already been on the path of serious Dharma practice for lifetimes, is born as a Chandala, beaten, and cast out experiencing poverty and scorn. Even the Bodhisattva couldn't escape difficulty.

Literal escape from difficulties may not be what the path of practice offers. Though if we cause less harm—and our practice surely helps us to do that—we're likely to suffer less harm in turn. But it can take a long time before the results of our new and wiser behaviors surface. It won't be immediate. It's just one more strand in the mix. The consequences of old, even ancient thoughts and deeds will continue to arise, causing difficulties. Freedom *from* difficulties is not the freedom we are going to find. Freedom to accept our karma fully is.

Painful things happen to all, good or bad. Life on this Earth, as the sutras say, is life on a *saha* world—life on a bearable or tolerable world, one suitable for Dharma practice, but not one always gloriously, radiantly wonderful. There *are* such worlds, sutras say, where beings never feel compelled to work on themselves, where the party of life is so great nothing more is called forth. No questioning arises. Tradition says that spiritually speaking, beings develop slowly on such worlds. Conversely, our saha world is not so overwhelmingly hellish and crushing that the transformative inner work we might do is beyond possibility. Sutras assert that such hell worlds also exist.

Our world is one on which spiritual practice is not just possible, but *reasonable*. There are clearly many worlds right here on Earth, heaven worlds and hell worlds. But in the middle place, this middle earth (if you will), this saha world, sutras say if we choose to work on ourselves, we can evolve more rapidly than in heavenly realms and with greater sureness and ease than in hellish ones. Not only *must* we develop wisdom and compassion here, we *can*. Our mixed realm is a place of opportunity where causes and conditions favorable to spiritual ripening are met. We know that it makes sense, given the actualities of life, to practice.

The jataka of Citta and Sambhuta shows that in his past lives the Buddha knew it, too. And that he, too, faced challenges in putting that knowledge into action. Yet, despite the difficulties, for him, too, persevering was the only sane response.

Over time determined efforts give way to something less self-conscious and self-willed. A sustained relationship with the falling away of body and mind in Zen practice becomes natural and normal. But as with learning to ride a two-wheeler, it takes effort, pedaling, bandages, training wheels, and someone we trust willing to run alongside for a time, before we're riding confidently on our own.

Here is where a teacher and a sangha, a community of fellow practitioners, come in. We need each other. And Dharma friendships persist through lifetimes—as this jataka shows. Not for the first time do healthy affinities emerge and trustworthy peers and guides appear. This, too, is a mystery, one that the jatakas attribute, as they do our difficulties, to the workings of karma, or cause and effect.

From the classical Buddhist view, difficulties come not as punishments and not randomly, but as ways of working through what we've created with our own past thoughts and deeds. Difficult situations can be ways of proving new skills and improving old responses. As we continue our zazen we gain the freedom to choose better responses to old problems. Painful situations still arise, but we now handle them less egotistically. This, in turn, creates better future karma.

In this jataka, the Buddha was born as a Chandala, the caste that was lowest of the low. He suffered rejection and abuse. Even though he opened the Dharma Eye, he suffered, seemingly unfairly. He became an outcast. He and his cousin practiced in the forest and died, unknown, unheralded, forgotten—and he the future Buddha! Though he had difficult karma, the jataka shows that aspiration and affinity for religious practice and awakening have nothing to do with our station in life.

The Sixth Patriarch of Zen, a great teacher, was said to have been poor and illiterate. Whether this is true or not (there is speculation that it is not), the archetype is clear: practice-realization is possible to all, for all. This is clear in the jatakas, right at the start of Buddhist tradition. Given the culture of India at the time, the jatakas offer what is, in a sense, a revolutionary, deeply democratic view. Birth has no bearing on one's potential. It's simply a matter of seeing a need to practice and, then, of practicing.

In this story the Bodhisattva died in a state of insight but that didn't remove the thorns and difficulties from his Path. He and his cousin and fellow Chandala practitioner were reborn as fawns and slain. They were hatched as osprey chicks and again slain. Talk about obstacles and difficulties! But then they were a chaplain's son and a king's son, the result of earlier perseverance in practice and eventually, one helping the other, they found their way to freedom.

It is not just an old tale. Persevering through difficulties, making choices, going on, finding opportunities, suffering injustices is our story, yours and mine. It is also the story of the Dalits, as members of the caste call themselves in India today. Though "untouchability" has been illegal since Independence, prejudice and discrimination, which include beatings, continue in rural areas. Dalits are converting to Buddhism in large numbers to change this, taking down remnants of the caste system. Old tales spring to life before our eyes.

In a life of ongoing practice doors open. Will we go through or not? If we do, will we keep going? The choice is ours, as is the need. Despite obstacles and difficulties, our mix of so-called "good" and "bad" karma, that's the good news. The need for us to work on ourselves is so obvious here, it's hard to avoid.

After the tale was told, the Buddha revealed that he had been the wise Citta and his cousin, Ananda, from whom the sutras come down to us, Sambhuta. They were still good friends. Yet even the Buddha and Ananda suffered the "slings and arrows of outrageous fortune." How does suffering end? Zen master Yüan-wu, who expanded the *Blue Cliff Record* into its final form, wrote, "The Diamond Sutra says, 'If you are about to drop into hell because of harmful karma in a previous life, then, because you are despised by others now, the harmful karma of your previous life will be extinguished.'"

Extinguishing harmful karma doesn't happen simply by going with the flow or bowing to an external fate. It also doesn't come just from being despised. Though acceptance is where freedom begins. Roshi Kapleau used to say that when painful things happen that we can't understand, we should put our palms together and say, "Thank you for this opportunity to work out old karma."

Eventually we see that it is the effort to be fully present that turns the tide, the effort of moment-by-moment counting of breath or awareness of breath, of attention to a koan point, or just fully sitting. In the midst of difficulties brought on by our old karma, Zen asks us to make an effort, sit up straight, and plumb the question beneath it to the bottom. That question is, "Where is our freedom now?" Not just "How can we one day be free, but how *are* we free right now?" Zen advises us not to sit back and wait to ask the future Buddha, Maitreya. Instead, in the ups, downs, losses, gains, betrayals, disillusionments, miscommunications, misunderstandings, joys, ailments, anxieties, errors, triumphs, and sorrows that *are* our life, each of us must and *can* find our answer—and our freedom.

The question that life puts before each of us—how in the midst of obstacles, difficulties, sufferings are we free right now?—is one Zen

deeply honors. Our tradition tells us that each being, including we ourselves, from the beginning have or are this perfect, whole, absolutely free
nature, buddha nature. This is reassuring, but it is also a challenge. If
this is so, where is it? Why don't we know it?

This question, this *quest*, is central not just to our practice, but to
our lives. In the midst of ups and downs as Chandalas, fawns, osprey,
ascetics, kings, queens, doctors, teachers, accountants, poets, cooks, gar-
deners, bakers, wise folk or fools, healthy or sick, humans or foxes our
answer and our practice are here or what use are they?

We bow to the Buddha and to our Dharma ancestors, women and
men named and unnamed who, troubled by questions of bondage and
freedom, by justice and injustice, nonetheless persevered and so entered
the Way. It is due to their efforts that our feet can be on the Path today.
Yet even the Bodhisattva had rough times. Without a roof to shelter him
from the burning sun, exposed to wind and rain, without a cradle to lie
in, he was set down in the dirt among the dogs. Having no home, his
mother nursed him as she anxiously hurried along the dusty highways.
Yet none of this put a stop to his thirst for the Way.

Life just as it is, with its warts and difficulties is *It*. Form is exactly emptiness, emptiness *exactly* form. This is the core of practice-realization,
the core of the realization of practice. Through all his many lives, the
Bodhisattva wanted so very much to fully awaken, fully realize mind
nature and become a full buddha. How many lives did he work at it?
How many lives did he *fail*? Was he dissatisfied throughout all those
thousands of jataka lives, only a fraction of which have been recorded
and identified, until he sat under the bodhi tree and saw the morning
star? If so, what a waste that would have been—all those lives, just so
many rungs on a ladder.

Rather, why not accept that all those varied lives (let's say five hundred of them, for convenience sake) were (as Zen master Wu-men says,
commenting about lives as a fox) not incomplete but, just as they were,

lives of grace? As Zen teaching and Dharma practice over time make clear, even a realized person, even a buddha cannot evade cause and effect.

At one point the Buddha tells his assembly that even as "the Buddha" he has ten sufferings, the remnants of deeply selfish deeds he himself had done very long ago, world ages ago. A summation of his illnesses and difficulties includes a variety of ailments including unhealed ulcerations and sores, headaches and migraines, rheumatism, periods of being lied about, not getting enough to eat, only getting the coarsest of grains as food, and living through six years of terrible hardship.

In other words, the Buddha didn't start off special or perfect. In an incalculably ancient past he'd been terribly deluded, burdened by heavy defilements, capable of making the most horribly selfish errors. But he changed. He made vows, practiced sincerely, kept going, accepted the consequences of all his own past errors, and did his very best.

The good news is that so can we.

Eleven

Great King Goodness: The Challenge of Nonviolence

Mahasilava Jataka, No. 51

The Bodhisattva, now a king of Varanasi named Goodness, delights in generosity, giving gifts to those in need. A wealthy minister steals a large sum from the king's treasury. When questioned, he gets angry, leaves, and goes to the neighboring kingdom of Kosala and tells that king that Goodness is weak.

The king of Kosala sends raiding parties to test this.

Three times King Goodness's men capture the raiders and each time Goodness tells them not to harm others, gives them gifts, and sends them home.

Convinced that King Goodness has been weakened by his commitment to goodness, the king of Kosala invades. King Goodness has a thousand champions ready to fight but orders them not to. The invaders capture the pacifist king and his champions and bury them to the neck in the graveyard, leaving them as food for jackals.

When the jackals come for fresh corpses, twice the king and his men scare them off with loud shouts. But the third time the jackals aren't scared away. The king then exposes his throat, as if offering his life to the jackal king, hoping for a quick death. When the jackal leader lunges, the king grabs his fur with his teeth, and the jackal's subsequent struggles loosen the dirt around the king.

The jackals flee. The king gets himself free and then frees the others. Two goblins fighting over a corpse lying in that graveyard across the boundary of their two territories ask the king to split it equally for them. With magic they bring him his bath, a meal, and then his sword. Raising his sword he splits the corpse perfectly. In gratitude, the goblins transport the Bodhisattva and his men back into the palace.

King Goodness strikes the sleeping usurper with the flat of his sword. Awakened, the king of Kosala, shocked by this turn of events, accepts that King Goodness wields a power greater than that of mere force of arms. He now vows to protect King Goodness and his realm.

Back on his throne King Goodness thinks, "How could any victory won by violence compare with this? I've saved my people and those of Kosala, too, from much suffering."

He tells all those gathered that even when the odds are long, it's worth persevering in goodness.

———◊———

The lotus blossoms bloom profusely in the fire.
—Buddhist saying

This exemplary jataka is more than a bit strange.

A leader's job is to protect, and on the national level this can mean rightfully waging a defensive war when necessary. But war is still *war*. Is there another way? The Bodhisattva-king not only believes there is, but is willing to go the limit to find out.

The Bodhisattva is determined to be a very good king. Indeed, his name proclaims it. He is King Mahasilava, that is, King "Great Goodness." With no desire to renounce his role in the world, he works to see it fulfilled as a Dharma Path. This is a wonderful model for lay practice: respect the life you have, the one your vows have brought you to, then do your best to confirm it as an expression of the Way.

This sounds good, but it's rarely easy.

How does one live ethically and kindly in a world where the three poisons of greed, anger, and ignorance run riot? Long ago the Buddha as King Goodness ran into this problem when his commitment to generosity and peace put him at odds with the realities of his times. And we can see that the challenges of our times are not so different from those long ago.

For one on the bodhisattva path, daily life is the context, the ground for embodying the perfections of character, *paramitas* that start with generosity and end with knowledge. Daily life and its responsibilities make the Way possible. Its challenges *are* the Way. They're not obstacles to the Way, nor are they in the way. Our lives with the ups and downs of career and family are not obstacles to a path of realization.

Here lies our challenge. Practice means practicing realization, realizing the nature of this life, this mind, this body, these thoughts and emotions.

Lay Dharma practice is not watered down monastic practice. It's its own form, built on recognition of diversity, not sameness. It's about actualizing practice in the midst of the "ten thousand things." As lay practitioners of Zen, we do less formal zazen and carry out less ceremony and liturgy than monastics, yet at the same time we have more opportunity to focus on essentials and integrate practice into the actualities of twenty-first-century life. Compassion, wisdom, and skillfulness mature through the challenges of work, family, and friendship. King Goodness shows us the Way. The challenge is the same: to realize *functioning* bodhisattva vows.

Our Path is here, now. This is where we muster the resolve to see deeply and find the placeless place we've never left. Practicing daily, we learn to shift our focus from wherever we mentally cling to *this* very breath, *this* count, this body-mind condition, this life situation. And so we come to see what's here and has always been here, perfect, complete, whole. "Dropping everything" doesn't mean lessening or losing commitments. It doesn't mean eliminating a thing called a "self" or ceasing participation in family, friendships, or work. What would that accomplish? What self would you "drop"? And who would do the dropping? Dropping everything means redirecting—at appropriate times—our attention from where it sticks, becoming present to what is, not to what we *think* is.

Zen asks: "What is here from before our parents were born? What is our Original Face?" To see past whatever clouds realization of this, we practice releasing attachment to dualistic views of self "in here" and other "out there." We shift our focus so that what's always here can show itself. Eventually we may learn to drop even dropping, letting go of, "I've got it! I've dropped dualistic views!" and even, "I've dropped thinking I've dropped dualistic views!"

If we stay alert, traces of realization are continually dropped. Dogen says that this ordinary life of traceless enlightenment continues endlessly. Looking like Buddhists is not the same as being Buddhists and doing the actual, demanding work of practice on the mat and integration practice in life. Seeing through our own delusive self-centered views is the core.

In this jataka King Goodness, while strong and compassionate, is an oddball, putting his kingdom at risk to uphold personal vows. The Bodhisattva's desire to give comes from earlier lifetimes and previous insights into the vast, pure, empty (of self-centered concepts) nature of reality. Compassion arises from this "emptiness"—which is not nothingness and not nihilism. Emptiness is quite lively, quite full.

Zen holds that generous, selfless behavior is the expression of our True Nature. Generosity is the nature of Original Mind and, if not blocked, will function. But usually to one degree or another it *is* blocked. "Don't do that! Put that down! Get away from the fire! Don't play in the street! Watch out! Be kind! Don't be silly! Take care of number one! Love yourself" can all be worthy bits of advice. Yet in times of great danger or stress they break down; doors open and selfless deeds walk in. Ordinary men and women do extraordinary things, lifting cars from accident victims, leaping in front of bullets, showing up to lend a hand. "Why or how did I do that?" we may wonder later. Even animals can astound us with acts of love, selflessness, and loyalty—the very things we like to imagine that make *us* human. True Nature means the nature of all beings. If a conditioned self is provisional, then all beings, including the Earth are our own body deserving of care. Yet to say, "I'll save them!" can drop us back into the dualistic soup.

There it is, the sickness of bodhisattvas. "The many beings are numberless; I vow to save them all," is the first of our Great Vows for All, the vows Zen practitioners recite after formal periods of zazen. The desire to save all beings, though urgent and essential, is in fact, also a kind of "sickness." If in reality there is nothing to call a separate "self" but only the arising of thoughts and feelings, the so-called "bundles" or *skandhas*, then going out of one's way to help an "other" is a kind of high-class error.

Buddhas, we are told, are so poor, so empty of self-centeredness that they're beyond even that. They eat, sleep, walk, brush their teeth, drink their coffee, read the newspaper, and drive their cars without self-conscious ideas of separation. Each act naturally, unselfconsciously brings refreshment and benefit to all. But bodhisattvas can't help *wanting* to give. For them it's not "Give me, give me, give me," the unconscious prayer wheel we mostly spin, but rather simply, "Give, give, give!"

Buddhism says the cosmos is alive, *is* Mind, and the nature of Mind is compassion and nondual prajna wisdom—which now and then we ourselves touch base with in our practice. Then there's just *this* tree, *this* cloud, *this* morning star. As Blake says, "If the doors of perception were cleansed, everything would appear, to man, as it is—Infinite"—or as itself. The Buddha realized this after six years and a trial-filled night of zazen when he glanced up and saw the morning star. Everything fell away, everything he'd thought of as himself was "gone, gone, entirely gone!" Just *star*! STAR! Tears flowed amid a kind of astonished silliness—"It was here the whole time and I never saw!" A morning star sat beneath the bodhi tree, all beings awake.

At such moments we ourselves *are* Goodness and only want to give. But who gives what to whom? The path of the bodhisattva is an effort of many lifetimes to answer this in doing, in action, in life. In the bodhisattva's lofty sickness of overwhelming love for every being, insect, person, star, and tree arising from deep realization of emptiness, from prajna nondual wisdom, there is still a self giving, still someone being excessively loving and kind.

After full awakening, after that last bit of self-centeredness fell away, wherever the Buddha looked he saw his own face looking back at him. Grass, bugs, river, star, all intimately alive! A morning star—the pupil of his own eye; a river, the flow of his own blood! He was at peace, settled, at home. Yet Buddhist tradition says that even Shakyamuni himself is still working at it. His great realization didn't lead to passivity in the face of others' troubles. Rather he spent his next fifty years doing his best to help and to teach. He created a sangha. He promoted nonviolence. He taught all, regardless of class or gender. In this tale the Bodhisattva who'll one day be that Buddha is still on the road, giving away stuff like mad, developing the will to sustain his practice through thick and thin, gaining "power for the Way."

In this jataka the good king suffers and the bad king doesn't. Then again, the worldly-wise king never experiences the Bodhisattva's joy. To reach that fulfilled moment, the Bodhisattva had to stay on the path, following the route of his own deepest nature. Yet it's not settled even for him until the end when his vow, after serious testing, finally comes through.

Wu-men says in his verse to case twenty in the *Gateless Barrier*: "If you want to know pure gold, you must perceive it in the midst of fire." The challenges of life are for us, as for the Buddha, where bodhisattva vows can be tested and matured. At the start of the tale King Goodness's vow is pure, but unconscious and naive. By the tale's end, through facing difficulties set in motion by that vow, it has become conscious and real.

Dharma practice begins as a resolve, a hope of transformation that we work on in the quiet of the meditation hall. Once set in motion, that vow and hope can and will continue to mature through the challenges of an ever more consciously lived life.

Twelve

The Monk Who Lied: Making Sense of Big Troubles

Losaka Jataka, No. 41

As a child, he who was to become the arhat, Losaka Tissa, was seen abandoned and starving on the streets of Varanasi by Sariputra, the Buddha's great disciple, who then brought him into the Buddhist Order. Yet, even when a grown man and an enlightened arhat, Losaka Tissa is never able to get a full meal. The food disappears as he's about to eat, or his begging rounds end up unsuccessful. Sariputra discovering this inability to ever get a full meal, arranges to make sure Losaka Tissa has one before death. Later, the monks ask why this was all so.

The Buddha tells them that in a previous world age, Losaka was a monk with some insight. Back then a new monk arrived and gave a talk that impressed the monastery patron. Then out of jealousy and fear of being displaced, Losaka Tissa kept notifications of meals as well as food offerings from the new monk, lied about it, and ate the food himself. The new monk, actually a deeply realized arhat of superb understanding, grasps what's happening and leaves, so as not to cause difficulties.

Too late, Losaka realizes his error. He then falls into despair over the shallow selfishness that led him to act foolishly and violate precepts. He dies and is reborn in lower realms for hundreds of thousands of years. Then he's reborn as an ogre for five hundred lives and only gets enough to eat one time. Reborn as a dog five hundred more lives, he, again, only gets enough to eat once.

After that, he's born into a family of beggars and given the name Mitta Vandaka. Later, when hardships increase in the village the signs all point to him, and he's eventually driven out.

In Varanasi he meets the Bodhisattva and joins his community, but only to get meals. He never takes the practice to heart and will not accept criticism or advice. He leaves the Bodhisattva and comes to a village where he marries a poor woman and has children. The king's anger falls on this village. Lots are drawn and, again, when all signs point to him he is forced out. He hires out as a deckhand on a ship that becomes becalmed. A divination of lots is used to see why the winds have died. Again, the signs point to him. The sailors make a raft and toss him onto the sea.

Drifting on the ocean he comes to islands with crystal palaces, silver palaces, gold palaces, jeweled palaces; with four goddesses, eight goddesses, sixteen goddesses, and thirty-two goddesses. Each time the goddesses must leave but tell him to wait, saying they'll soon return. Instead, he sails away seeking *better* islands, better palaces, more beautiful goddesses.

He lands on an island of ogres and, hungry, grabs a goat to make a meal. But the goat is actually an ogress in disguise who grabs him instead, and hurls him over the sea. He lands in a thornbush outside Varanasi.

He sees another goat and thinks: "Grabbing a goat got me here. Maybe grabbing another will get me back to those goddesses. I was a fool to leave." He grabs the goat and the goatherds laying in wait to catch a goat thief, grab him.

In taking him to the king for punishment they pass the Bodhisattva with his five hundred students. The Bodhisattva says, "He's one of mine." They release him to the Bodhisattva. After that Mitta Vandaka, humbled and receptive, stays with his teacher and works sincerely at the practice.

The Buddha says to his monks, "Losaka Tissa was himself both the cause of his getting little and the cause of his gaining arhatship."

———◊———

He must tightly grasp the rope and not let it go,
For the ox still has unhealthy tendencies.
      —*The Ten Ox-Herding Pictures*, "Catching the Ox."

Though we can't evade cause and effect—the functioning of karma—we can accept and awaken to it, realize its empty ground, and not see past lives but really look at our present one. Then, even in the midst of difficulties we find a degree of freedom. This is not the freedom we might have naively hoped for, not, "Yippee! I can do anything I want! I'm free!" But realistically we can say, "I can now live with some peace and dignity in the midst of difficulties and changes."

The tale of Losaka Tissa starts with a lengthy introductory "story of the present," about his early life as an impoverished, abandoned child, and his inability, even as an enlightened elder in the Buddhist Order, to get a full meal. Then it moves on to the complex tale of past lives. The tale resonates with Homer's *Odyssey*—rafts on the ocean, goddesses, islands, homecoming. The story might be old enough to have wandered into the tale of Jonah who also gets tossed overboard when lots are drawn—or vice versa. Regardless, we have to respect this headstrong guy for repeatedly leaving glamour and pleasure to head out again onto the vast empty sea. The mind of practice is still with him. "Arouse the mind without its abiding, anywhere," said the Buddha. And Mitta Vandaka, as he's known in that past life, does that. He keeps going.

The good news is that Losaka Tissa matures through the fire of his sufferings and becomes able to transcend his difficulties. The kindness of Sariputra in the "story of the present" that leads into the jataka proper is deeply human. He's the one who sees this starving child, Losaka, and brings him into the sangha. Later, when Losaka is himself an enlightened arhat, Sariputra gets him his first—and simultaneously last—full meal, just before he dies. Sariputra emerges as a greatly human being.

Enlightenment confers nothing we don't already have. It doesn't make us better, special, or freer from life's pains. In that long ago past life, he who had been the Elder Losaka Tissa had insight. Yet the self-created, ego-centered pain of being overlooked or shown up caught and held him. Old habits die hard.

After a long meditation retreat, when we go back into the events and responsibilities of our ordinary lives we can feel transparent, like visitors from another planet or travelers from the future. It doesn't necessarily make things easier. Sometimes things can seem harder for a while. "Freedom" can mean being stripped free of illusions. Without habitual buffers, we see more clearly. What is beautiful is truly so, and what is mean, ugly, painful, and pain-producing can no longer be ignored. Getting clearer means we'll see beauties, errors, and terrors more keenly. What used to be overlooked no longer can be. We can't help but pay attention because it is the nature of Mind to be aware. Through practice we gain equanimity, the ability to see and experience things more steadily. Not getting thrown or becoming immediately defensive, we gain the freedom to act more skillfully.

Elder Losaka Tissa doesn't say, "I'm an enlightened elder in the Buddha's Order. I deserve a full meal!" Instead, he comes to the placeless place of peace despite a headstrong, misguided, self-centered past. He gets there by his own efforts: "This Losaka was himself the cause both of his getting little and of his gaining arhatship." Who we are is both cause and effect of what we do and have done—what we ourselves do and do not do is the core. Yet, though it's fundamentally up to us ourselves, we don't go at it alone. We have sanghas, teachers, places of practice.

Koun Yamada Roshi said that the purpose of Zen is the perfection of character, but he wasn't teaching self-help or self-improvement. The perfecting he spoke of comes from seeing our situation truly and realizing that, in reality, there is *ultimately* no inner person forever terribly and irrevocably separate from the ten thousand things—moon, stars, bugs, wind, animals, trees, mountains, rivers, people. And, so, there is ultimately no one to benefit from self-centeredness, no one who needs to take life's irritations and turn them into tragically silly behaviors. When attachment to this little self is dropped, released, seen through even a bit, there is just this pain in the knee, this laugh outside the window, this whoosh of wind in the trees, this whir of the fan. The linking of thoughts into a sequence, the endless looping that creates an inner, separate-seeming "person," the so-called "Mind road," is cut off. Each moment is present. Blake says, "One thought fills immensity." Through ongoing practice such moments can become the foundation of a fully present, conscious life.

When people would complain to Roshi Kapleau saying, "What did I do to deserve this?" he, no stranger to troubles himself, would answer, "Plenty." If we are the cause of our difficulties, while sobering, it's good news. We can also be the cause of our liberation.

So why not take up the way of practice? And, if we do, why let small irritations and inconveniences put a stop to what might be achieved? We get up in the morning, perhaps earlier than we wish, and sit in zazen. We rise from sitting to go to work and to work on ourselves, putting in place what we've realized. We may be anxious before a meeting with a teacher, but we go and discover we can, despite anxiety, emerge into clearer space.

We work to uphold and embody precepts and paramitas in the events, trials, tribulations, and joys of our lives, no longer content to drift. We are awake in the stream.

This doesn't mean we should force ourselves to push against what is or disdain what feels right. That kind of thinking leads to punishing the self rather than realizing the Self. The Buddha found that asceticism was a dead-end, not a way of liberation.

How will we walk the Middle Way of wholeness that the Buddha taught? The old teachers say it's relatively simple: practice regularly. Roshi Kapleau used to say that ten minutes a day, every day, is better than two hours one day and nothing for the next three. Respect your practice. Sitting on the mat is our version of the Buddha sitting beneath the bodhi tree. It is where we wake up, becoming present to sounds, smells, sensations, birdcalls, traffic noises, sunlight, and shadow. Seeing more clearly, being more present, we respect whatever we encounter. As Dogen says in his advice to the cook, pots and pans should be respected—they are our body.

Let us also own up to our mistakes and, when necessary, do what needs doing to heal the past and improve the future. This is what the Bodhisattva does in the jatakas as he faces his errors and the unskillful actions of others. Finally, keep at it. While it might be easy to talk about, it can still be hard to do. Hard to get up early, difficult to forgo things we might otherwise want. Dharma practice is not immediately convenient. In the beginning—which might mean years and can include decades and lifetimes—it may take self-conscious effort. The mind is slippery, said to be like trying to grasp a hollow gourd bobbing on a stream. Over and over we lose attention and may try to grasp our practice, shut everything out, and cling to it rather than embody it. There are also times we simply lose it, give way to old emotional storms, and wander back into self-centeredness where we make stupid mistakes.

We're not alone. A Zen layman back in T'ang China, a noted poet and governor of a province, visited a Zen master who had the habit of doing zazen up in a tree and asked, "What's the essence of the Buddha Way?" The Master answered, "Do good. Avoid evil. Save the many beings." T'ang China being the golden age of Zen, and those answers being the Mahayana version of the three general resolutions of classical Buddhism, the governor replied, "Any child of three knows that." The master replied, "But a man of seventy can still find it hard to fully practice it."

It's good to remember that while we might not find practice convenient, we may also discover that it's vital.

Thirteen

The Brave Parrot: Being Small in a Big, Troubled World

*Adaptation by the author,
precise Pali source unknown*

The Buddha was once a little gray parrot.

When lightning sets a tree ablaze and her forest begins to burn, the parrot cries out a warning to others, "Fire! Run to the river!" Then she flies toward the safety of the river and its other shore.

But as she flies, she sees below her animals and trees already trapped, surrounded by flames. And suddenly she sees a way to save them. She flies to the river. The animals already huddled safely there are sure nothing more can be done. Each offers a valid reason for staying safely put where they are and not making further efforts. But the little parrot says she has spotted a way, so she must try.

She wets her feathers in the river, fills a leaf cup with water, and flies back over the burning forest. Back and forth she flies carrying drops of water. Her feathers become charred, her claws crack, her eyes burn red as coals.

A god looking down sees her. Other gods laugh at her foolishness, but this god changes into a great eagle, flies down, and tells her, as it's hopeless, to turn back. She won't listen but continues bringing drops of water. Seeing her selfless bravery, the god is overwhelmed and begins to weep. His tears put out the fire and heal all the animals, plants, and trees. Falling on the little parrot, the tears cause her charred feathers to grow back red as fire, blue as a river, green as a forest, yellow as sunlight.

She is now a beautiful bird.

The parrot flies happily over the healed forest she has saved.

———— ◊ ————

Lead, kindly fowl! They always did: ask the ages. What bird has done yesterday man may do next year, be it fly, be it moult, be it hatch, be it agreement in the nest.

—James Joyce, *Finnegan's Wake*

The Brave Parrot Jataka embodies the central bodhisattva vow of Mahayana Buddhism—to save, that is, liberate, all beings from suffering. As Mahayana Buddhists we vow to free all who suffer in the bondage caused by ignorance of True Nature. We also vow to release beings from the bondage we ourselves impose on them by our own inattention and ignorance—which also means we vow to liberate rivers, mountains, plants, oceans, animals, and fellow humans from the effects of exploitive social and economic systems.

Saving all beings is the first of the "Four Great Vows for All" known to all aspiring buddhas and bodhisattvas past, present, and future. The three remaining vows are actualizations of the first: to let go of our own habitual greed, anger, and ignorance; to recognize everything we encounter as a potential Dharma gate opening onto deeper understanding; to wholeheartedly undertake the impossible task of fully embodying the ungraspable, selfless Way of the Buddha. In other words, in order to fulfill the Great Vow to save all, we must do the hard—one might even say *impossible*—work of fully waking up.

The little parrot in this jataka finds herself at a crossroads. She is capable of saving herself, but recognizes this is not enough.

At the beginning of the story the little parrot is content with her life. She has the gift of flight, after all. She is even happier at the end, having used her gift not just for her own sake but to liberate others. Her own great vow has become that much more real.

Greed, hatred, and ignorance arise in our minds, and if we build a self on them, we're trapped. But if we don't make our nest there, then, though self-centered thoughts come, they also go like the wind that shakes the branches and is gone. We don't fight them; we don't try to stop them. We breathe into them, attend to our practice in the midst of them, and so see them arise and fade. We accept our impermanence nakedly, directly, freely.

As we become freer of our own stuckness, we free others from what we ourselves no longer project onto them. To be free *of* ourselves is to free others *from* ourselves, from the burden of having to bear and bear with our needs, desires, and expectations. To free others is to diminish our fascination with the experience of isolated egotism. What is around us enters us and, as Dogen says, intimately confirms us. The two go hand in hand. Our work, the work of practicing realization, lies here.

This practice can and indeed must be taken up where we are, as we are; otherwise our vow remains just a distant ideal. This vow is not a formality, not simply something we recite after periods of zazen. Each day we do our best to dip in the river and fly back with a few drops of water for our burning world. Each day we practice the realization of this moment and engage this never-to-be-repeated moment of practice.

The text for the Brave Parrot Jataka remains elusive. It exists as a few lines of verse in the brief "Jatakastava"—"Verses in Praise of the Buddha's Former Lives"—a short Scythian-Khotanese text from just prior to 1000 CE. Though this speaks of a partridge who out of compassion for all, heroically gets water to quench a conflagration, it is seen as a variant of the parrot jataka. The full story does not appear in either the Pali *Jataka* or the Sanskrit *Jatakamala*, though jataka number 35 in the Pali collection of 547 about a little quail who stops a forest fire with an act of truth is also seen as a variant. An original seems to also exist as a carving at the Buddhist monument of Borobudur as well as in a painting at the Ajanta Caves.

Whether as text or visual art, the ending of that story in which all are saved and the forest restored is different from our synopsis above: the god, moved by the parrot's heroism, doesn't burst into tears. Instead, he squeezes a cloud causing rain to fall. I created the god's tears version when I began telling this tale not long after I read the original. The colors of the parrot's feathers came later as well.

The essence is that deeds make us who we are. There is truth greater than fact. Myth reveals what never was but always is. While fact recounts what happens in one time, in one place, myth ideally reveals the archetype—what happens in all times, all places. Literalists sticking to facts can still create a truncated and, thus, false story.

Stories must find their relevance for each generation or they wither and fade. I chose to make the parrot female. The feminine is reawakening. Like so much of the preserved classical Buddhist tradition, the jatakas are often, though not exclusively, patriarchal. It's true that there are wise women, enlightened nuns, and true wives and queens, but rarely, if ever, does the Buddha appear as female. Perhaps monastic forms led to the suppression of a greater truth. In the jatakas, the Buddha could be a crow, a mongrel dog, or a monkey, but *never* a woman? I found that a little hard to take.

One last personal modification: I added other animals. They entered the story when I wrote a version for children. I liked the animals and they liked the story, so they stayed. The parrot is not the fastest, gentlest, or mightiest animal—but the race is not always to the swiftest. The parrot's gift of flight has unforeseen consequences. From above she gains an encompassing view. Looking down she can see how bad things really are in her forest home. Expanded vision is the gift of flight in addition to swift travel. The parrot sees the big picture, has *vision*. That first iconic photo of the Earth from space changed us. Suddenly we were all little parrots. Let's not underestimate that gift.

We each have an original gift as well. Zen master Hakuin writes in his "Song in Praise of Zazen": "From the beginning all beings are Buddha." "From the beginning" means it is ours from the start. We will not gain it, will not become more of it, and will not lose it. But what, in fact, is *it*? And why don't we know *it*?

We may know shame, guilt, fear, and inadequacy. We may get caught by an inflated, overly confident ego or by an overly self-critical defensive one. They are a pair, after all. Yet either can become the irritating grit under the hard shell of the ego-oyster that may in time produce a pearl. Why don't we know who or what we really are? How are we—just as we are, stuck and limited as we are—buddhas? This works on us without cease or pause and ultimately, if we accept the practice it encourages, to our benefit. It, too, is a gift.

From the start the little parrot was a happy bird. What can we do to be happy birds? Should we ignore difficulties, shut our eyes to life's sorrows, and wear rose-colored glasses? Should we accept whatever happens and call it kismet or fate? The little parrot doesn't think so. She smells smoke and responds, crying out: "Fire! Fire! Run to the river!" Flapping her wings, she flies away.

"Right, right!" say the old teachers. If you can be free of danger, do what you need to get free. Don't sit there moaning over your sad state, rehearsing "what ifs." And let's accept, too, that being present in some situations is going to mean, "Get going! Get out of there!" The Buddha does that in the Wise Quail Jataka when quarrels put his flock at risk. Being awake in our lives and in our practice means, "respond!"

In koan number fourteen of the *Blue Cliff Record*, a monk asks, "What is the teaching which Shakyamuni preached throughout his life?" Yün-men answers, "One preaching in response!" That's it! The key, of course, lies in where the response comes from. A self-centered response won't do.

Kapleau Roshi used to say that being a Buddhist doesn't mean acting *like* Buddha, imitating the guy on the altar with the half-smile on his lips. If you're at a party sitting in a corner with crossed legs, wearing a halo, looking wise and kind, Roshi might say, "Get up and dance! Try the hors d'oeuvres. Talk to people." In short, respond to time, place, and circumstance. When sad things happen, we're going to cry. When joyous things happen, we'll laugh. When infuriating things happen, we might even get angry. "Selflessness" doesn't mean we become like zombies or that we're blown about by every wind. The Dharma practice of releasing or seeing through self-centeredness leads to a fuller, more centered, and more fully present life.

The practice of counting this breath, experiencing this breath, and shifting attention from our compulsive internal narrative allows the *vroom* of the passing car, the *caw* of the crow, the ache in our knee, the blue of the sky to say it all.

Zen master Dogen teaches that to reach our potential there's no need to push ourselves forward to become one with the ten thousand things. Rather, getting out of the way, we let the ten thousand things be us, confirm us, take their rightful place *as* us, enlightening us with intimacy. Master Dogen adds that to push the self forward to become one with the ten thousand things is called delusion. When the ten thousand things step in confirming the self, it is called realization or enlightenment. We don't get something called "enlightenment"; rather, we momentarily release self-centeredness to re-find our original intimacy with bugs, clouds, people, cars, trash, crows.

The compassion that arises from intimacy isn't sentiment; it's action. Samantabhadra, the bodhisattva of selfless activity, rides a powerful elephant and nothing can deter his—or her—compassionate activity. Ultimately, it is our nature to be brave parrots. It is our nature to see possibilities and act on them. It is not the things we try and fail at that later torment us, but the things we might have done but didn't. Poems we didn't write, paintings we didn't paint, loving words left unsaid, journeys not taken, zazen put off, knots left still tied, kind deeds not done—these are what disturb our sleep.

Through daily practice we find the habitual self no longer a monolithic thing. Our path is not one of gaining new Buddhist beliefs, but of seeing more deeply into the nature of what we already are. We are not saved by becoming more "Buddhist" or by gaining a better self. We don't get rid of ourselves, but letting go and losing ourselves, we find ourselves as if for the first time. Whatever milestones we have attained, there are others to come—if we keep going.

The brave little parrot shows the way. Through past work she's gained karmically hard-won wings and can fly to safety. She could rest on the other shore and be safe—but what of others? What of the animals and trees already surrounded by flames? When the Buddha in a past life was the Banyan Deer the thought, "What of others?" kept him from claiming his own freedom. He was tested again and again. "Leave? I can't until the other herd is free, until all beasts are free, until all birds, and fish, too, are safe. Only then can I be free." In the Hungry Tigress Jataka, the Bodhisattva as a prince might have walked past the starving tigress and her cubs, only he didn't. As a hare, the Bodhisattva saw a starving beggar and, in response to a plea for food, leapt into the fire. He couldn't walk by.

Neither can the Bodhisattva as the little parrot fly to a place of personal safety. Though she's just a bird, she sees a way to help. Seng-ts'an in *Verses on the Faith Mind* says, "When picking and choosing are cast aside, the Way stands clear and undisguised." There is no ground left for the little parrot to pick and choose. Everything has been taken: home, security, friends, trees, air. All is smoke and fire. And then when all is gone, she *sees*.

What does the parrot see that makes the Way clear and undisguised? From high up she sees how all is connected; trees, river, mountains. From up high, she sees far. But she sees beyond even that. She sees intimately and knows the forest as herself. This no-seeing is transformative: when the mind of the bodhisattva is awakened, seeing is doing. The ancient grit of "me and my" that stands like a veil between our seeing and doing, is "gone, gone, entirely gone" as the *Heart of Perfect Wisdom Sutra* says.

Where we are is where we take up the practice. Where we are is where we focus on the moment. "Crossing the stream" comes down to our work right now—simple, yet hard to do. Attention strays. And off we go with it, floating away from this profoundly present moment.

The little parrot stays steady. Having touched the Other Shore, she puts together a vivid new scenario. Making brilliant, spontaneous use of her circumstances—wings, fire, river—she forms anew the story of the vow of the bodhisattva, a tale told in action not words. This vow that she, the Bodhisattva, has been working on for lifetimes is the deepest reality of her mind. It is the reality of every mind. The great vow to save the many beings can be worked on and embodied precisely because it is already who we are.

This is the paradox that Dogen agonized over: why did all the sages of the past have to work so hard to realize enlightenment if buddha nature is already who we are? He struggled on and on until self-conscious awareness of body and mind fell away. Because of enlightened nature, because of primal-vow mind, we, too, can work on realizing enlightened nature and experiencing innate vow mind. This vow carries the parrot over the flames of her burning world on wide wings. It carries us forward in our practice as well.

Bodhisattvas don't make escaping from the flames of this world the point of their practice. They live in the middle of the stream, flying daily over the burning forest, dipping into the cool waters of emptiness. They don't give up, and they don't settle down saying, "That's enough. I'll build my comfy nest here." They keep bringing what they can—a little talent, a little insight, a little water as few and as tiny as those drops may be. Yet how each sparkles! There it is! There it is! Cool and refreshing! Then *phhht!* it, too, is gone.

Yet, says this old story, if we keep going, keep flying, keep practicing, things that logic can't predict can happen. Who, after all, *is* the Bodhisattva? Does the story just recount an ancient exploit from Shakyamuni's personal route to Buddhahood? Look again. The beauty of Zen lies in this question: *Who?*

Our world is burning. Trees, animals, ecosystems, and social safety nets are being engulfed every day. The causes are exactly as the Buddha said 2,600 years ago—greed, anger, and ignorance of our own nature. Our practice is not about inspecting our navels, simply trying to calm our distress. Brave parrots, if you love your forest, flap your wings, find a way to the river, and do not give up: when the chips are down and the last hand has been played, sometimes the inexplicable occurs. A god descends, clouds burst, tears fall, and suddenly all is whole and well. For a moment we become what we are and have always been.

And then we can really get to work.

Fourteen

The Quarreling Quails: Arguments and Anger on the Path

Sammodamana Jataka, No. 33

Long ago the Bodhisattva was a quail and the leader of a large flock. A hunter learns to imitate the birds' calls and begins trapping them. The Bodhisattva-quail, noticing some of his birds are missing, puts two and two together, gathers his community, and warns them of the hunter. He instructs them that if they find themselves trapped, to stick their heads out through the net and, flapping their wings in unison, work together and fly away.

"Leaving the net draped on a bush," he adds, "you can drop beneath it and fly to freedom. Working together keeps us free."

His advice works—for a time. Then birds start arguing. The Bodhisattva notices, calls another gathering, and says that they should go deeper into the forest where they can practice their skills in safety till they get it right.

Some birds say, "There's no need. You taught us what to do."

Others say that they won't go, as "This is where we've always lived."

Others add, "We're comfortable here."

The Bodhisattva gathers those willing to go farther and flies deeper into the forest. When the hunter's net falls on those that stay, instead of working together, they begin arguing about who should lead the escape. As they argue, the hunter carries them off.

The birds that went with the Bodhisattva continue to work on their skills. When arguments arise, they end quickly.

Working together they stay free.

———◇———

If you argue right and wrong, you are a person of right and wrong.
—Zen master Wu-men

You can win a verbal battle, but still lose something. Nonetheless there are times when we must work to uphold right and beneficial views and see wrong ones—selfish, narrow, destructive ones—exposed and cast out. Everything from fairy tales to hard-boiled thrillers explore our hope of actualizing this archetype. The good guys win! Mordor crumbles! The Death Star is destroyed!

The desire to see the world clarified, all things clearly identified for what and as they are seems universal. Unfortunately, it doesn't happen much outside stories.

In Zen practice, milestones come when we see so clearly we can't help but laugh aloud. At such times the Way "stands clear and undisguised," as the *Verses on the Faith Mind*, says. There is no argument, no way to argue. Clear is clear. Absolutely!

Still, our ordinary lives are often full of doubt, confusion, miscommunication, and disagreement. Which lead to arguments, with "I'm right!" "No! I'm right!" at the core. Arguments are not simply a waste of time. Israeli poet Yehuda Amichai says (as translated by Stephen Mitchell and Chana Bloch): "From the place where we are right / flowers will never grow / in the spring."

There may, indeed, be a right perspective and right outcome, but *argument* may not be the path to get us there. In fact, argument can take the right view and squash, scramble, or destroy it. The power of argument is intense, like an undertow or rip tide. One minute we're swimming for shore, the next fighting for our life against a current dragging us out to sea.

When entangling nets fall, weapons are drawn, and sharp words fly, it won't do to put on the buddha smile, cling to a halo, or try to recall that article on meditation we just read. A halo and half-smile can themselves be weapons wielded to maintain our sense of superiority. Sangha practice strengthens us by taking such supports away. We take refuge in the Three Treasures—Buddha, Dharma, Sangha. The invisible support we experience in the extended sitting of multiday sesshin or retreat is an example of the power of sangha. Even daily zazen of two or three rounds becomes simpler when we join our practice with others. Together we accomplish what one alone never could.

And yet, given ordinary schedules of family and work, sitting alone is going to be a regular expression of our path. Not to worry—solitary zazen is a good way to discover our strengths and embody personal aspirations. One of our challenges as lay practitioners is to find a healthy balance between solo and community practice.

We may also know from experience that when communal life goes wrong it can be worse than a nightmare of aloneness. The potential for community, for sangha, lies at the heart of every group. When it fails, there is an odor of rot. What we sense is the decay of what might have been, the lost life of the stillborn community that should have formed but didn't. Some groups, like some relationships, are toxic, and then our best response might be to walk away.

Sitting in zazen on our own then can be like a gleam of heaven. Still, we are social beings and most of us will miss companionship. So we reenter the stream of life, searching for real community, not just another group.

In the Quail jataka, sangha practice is central, and working together in harmony, crucial—and this is not simply idealistic. As the tale shows, group life also means potential conflict, and conflict makes us vulnerable. When harmony is lost, we are in danger.

Yet suppressing differences to have "peace" is no solution either. We get cliques, factions, whisperings, seethings, and periodic boilings. Worse, pointless argument means the reassertion of egotism, the very thing we aim to see through and get at least a bit free of in ongoing meditation practice. Once argument starts, the mind of attention is lost. The ox breaks its halter and runs off to painfully familiar haunts. This can be the destruction of the sangha jewel. In losing ourselves to anger and self-will, we can lose what we hold dear, as well as what we aim to accomplish. Yet such moments can seem unavoidable. If we can't stop ourselves, then backing off and taking ourselves out of it for a time might be wise.

It's not enough to sit and meditate and experience calm, silence, and peace—as good as those things are (and they are very good indeed). Without them chaos, violence, and anxiety easily reign. But we must stand up, walk out of the zendo, and *actualize* the Way in our life, not just talk about it, not just make the meditation hall into a place to hide out from a crazed and crazy world.

We *are* the Way. It is not outside us. It is not something to run to or cling to, point to or proselytize about.

So if we *are* the Way, how do we respond when alternate views clash with our own? What does nonviolence mean then? Saying, "It's all One" and letting it go, won't do. That might work in a domestic squabble where a base of love, respect, and trust is already in place, just temporarily hidden. Then some form of "We're both wrong; let's call a halt" might help realign us.

But how about when the argument is about climate change, gender equality, Wall Street bailouts, health care, government shutdown, gun control, evolution, election tampering, immigration reform, or the Middle East?

Jonathan Swift was outraged by our proclivity to take pet beliefs as gospel and be willing to kill those who don't share them. Swift's was a wrathful-deity Dharma anger, not personal or petty, and he showed it clearly in his writing. At one point his creation, Gulliver, comes to a place where wars are fought over whether to open a soft-boiled egg from its pointed or round end. Each view has adherents and bloody wars are waged over this ridiculous "truth." But righteous outrage is no excuse for self-righteousness.

Swift gave sermons and wrote books. He didn't physically attack those who cut their eggshells differently than he. How quickly does our blood boil? And why? We should find out. Yet, there are places where we must take a stand and say no or yes and mean it—and these might not entail *argument*. Gandhi didn't argue with the British. He fought non-violently against them. The Warsaw Ghetto rose against the Nazis and battled valiantly to the end with smuggled weapons. There was no way to leave or talk a way out. It wasn't an argument.

Harada Roshi, the twentieth-century Japanese Soto Zen monk whose Rinzai koan work became the foundation for much of the contemporary koan practice in the West, admitted that if it hadn't been for his Zen practice, with his hot temper he might have eventually killed someone. But harnessed to *bodhichitta*, a yearning to know and embody the Way for the sake of all, his temper became fuel for a Dharma fire. He used it rather than being used by it. In this tale, the Bodhisattva saw what was going on, held meetings to present his view, and pointed out consequences. He asked for support and for acknowledgment of truth. When that failed, he saw what needed to be done and did it.

When things aren't right and can't be made right, perhaps the wisest thing is to pack bags and depart. Rather than fighting, leaving the field of battle might be kindest. Once the Buddha, tiring of some rancorous dispute in the sangha, withdrew to the forest to practice alone. He'd had enough. It was also his teaching for that situation. "Get on with your practice," he was saying. "Time waits for no one."

As we see in other jatakas, the Bodhisattva was discerning. He didn't apply leaving as his one-stop answer to life's dilemmas. Most of the time perseverance in the right for the right was his preferred mode. The Buddha was of the warrior caste. In many jatakas the spirit of digging in and holding on or of moving forward into headwinds was how he embodied his aspiration to save all beings. In this jataka he is also wise enough to recognize that fruitless effort leads to loss of energy, integrity, and purpose—as well as, potentially, life—so he moves on.

Such experiences can be difficult and painful. And they can be absolutely right, a way to uphold the precepts and embody the Way. If that time comes, there's no need to argue. We pack our bags and leave. Isn't this the central point of zazen? We leave the flow of habitual self-centered thought. We leave the central delusion of self "in here" and others "out there." We leave it all!

This jataka is not just encouragement toward future points of practice. It embodies the fulfillment/realization of "right now!" In zazen we "right now!" drop self-centeredness and leave our old accumulations of ideas, worn-out thoughts, dusty hopes and dreams and let them go. This is flying farther into the wild forest always accessible to us beyond the tangle of argument. It is here, now, open to us with each breath, each round of zazen, each retreat. Arguing can stop; the anciently held-to and believed-in-as-fully-real inner dialogue can halt. We can be free of the box of the skull, the nets of *yes* and *no*, *right* and *wrong*. Then what remains? What have we been failing to see as we argue away, day in, day out? Step up and say a true word! The sun is rising, shining on green leaves! This looks like a good spot. Let's settle the flock here.

Tradition says, that the Quail jataka was told by the Buddha in the Banyan Grove, near Kapilavastu, his hometown. He told it to nobles of his own Shakya clan upon learning that a minor disagreement over a porter's head pad had led, not only to arguments, but to a very real possibility of war.

This little jataka then was a cautionary tale told by the Buddha for the sake of his own family. His aim was to save lives.

Perhaps the next time argument looms it might help save ours as well.

Fifteen

The Bodhisattva Robber: What's Right, What's Wrong?

Satapatta Jataka, No. 279

Long ago, the Bodhisattva was the leader of a robber gang.

A man who'd lent money to a distant villager dies. His wife, dying, too, tells their son to get the money they're owed. The boy heads off and does so, then starts for home. Meanwhile, the Bodhisattva and his robber gang are lying in wait along a forest road, looking for travelers to rob.

When the boy enters the forest and starts walking along the road, a snarling jackal appears and blocks his way, as if trying to prevent him from going farther. "A mad jackal!" he thinks and, picking up stones to throw, drives it away. The boy walks on.

A crane, flying overhead and seeing the boy, calls out loudly. "A good sign!" thinks the boy, and looking up, thanks the crane. Then the robbers spring from hiding and grab him.

The Bodhisattva asks, "Do you carry money from some loan repayment?"

"How do you know?" stammers the boy.

"Were your parents ill?" asks the Bodhisattva.

"Yes. My father died, and my mother is quite sick. I'm hurrying home to her now."

The Bodhisattva says, "I understand the language of birds and beasts. Your mother has already died. She was that little jackal trying to stop you from going farther and was warning you that robbers were hiding just ahead. That crane wasn't your friend and wasn't wishing you well. It was actually announcing that you carried money from a loan repayment and, so, were ripe for robbing. It must have been your enemy in a past life. Go home and hold a service for your parents. Don't make assumptions. Pay better attention in the future. You got it all wrong."

Though his men protest, he lets the boy, and his money, go.

———◊———

And now I will tell how it first came about that Robin Hood fell afoul of the law.

—Howard Pyle

In this jataka, the Bodhisattva is a robber. In another jataka (number 265 in the Pali collection), he fights against robbers and drives them off. That jataka is about a merchant with a five-hundred-wagon caravan who hires the Bodhisattva, then a forester, to guide them through a forest. Halfway through, five hundred robbers attack, and the men of the caravan throw themselves down in terror—except for the Bodhisattva. Shouting, leaping, and dealing blows left and right, he puts all five hundred thieves to flight, then guides the caravan to safety. Once safely through the forest, the merchant asks, "What's your secret? When everyone was overcome, you alone stood up to the attackers and drove them off. It would be a good secret to know."

The Bodhisattva says, "I have no secret. I had a job to do. Having sworn to protect you, I resolved to keep my word. I didn't cling to life but used it to fulfill my purpose."

In that story, his teaching is clear: forget yourself and much can be accomplished, stay trapped in a habitual sense of who and what you are, and you limit your potential. One person fighting five hundred is sometimes used in Zen as a metaphor for the vigor and resolve of active zazen, so this has connotations with meditation practice as well. Amid distractions, wandering thoughts, and self-involved concerns that, like robbers, can steal our attention and make us lose the riches of this moment, our job is to stay focused and alert. But, vigor and resolve don't necessarily mean tension or strain. Awareness doesn't require force. In the early years of practice this can seem paradoxical. When learning any new skill—and awareness is a skill—in the beginning we can fumble, overreach, and push too hard. It's part of the normal learning curve. If we persist, in time our practice willingly joins us in our lives and is also content to sit quietly with us on the mat.

The forester jataka reminds us that if we shift our focus from the habitual, self-centered self, then, even as countless thoughts arise, we're like a person who single-handedly faces and deals with hordes of foes. Courage, wisdom, and compassion boil down to one tasty brew. Releasing our death grip on self-centeredness, everything we meet gains richness and flavor.

In the jataka in which the Bodhisattva is the robber, a woman dies and immediately takes form as a little jackal to try to stop her child from walking into danger. Selfless love allows a mother to do the seemingly impossible.

There is a jataka in which the Bodhisattva is a horse in the service of a king. The kingdom is invaded, and the horse goes to war. He breaks through the enemy ranks six times, capturing six kings. In the last encounter he is badly wounded. When they remove his armor to put it on a fresh mount, the Bodhisattva-horse says, "Leave it. I am determined. No other horse can do it. I mean to end this war." And he goes off, captures the final king, returns—and dies.

He has given his life, beyond self-concern. Dogs, horses, elephants, dolphins, chimpanzees, even cats have been recorded doing what certainly look like courageous, selfless things. Yet how many of us fear that when our time comes to step up we might freeze and end up groveling like the merchant's men? Young men can suffer deeply from such doubt and put on bold fronts or take crazy risks to hide it. Yet they can still wonder, "If such and such happened, would I be strong or brave enough to do the right thing?" And they may push themselves recklessly into danger to find out, or to bury the fear.

Forgetting the self, paintings are painted, poems are written, plays are made on the ball field, neighbors are helped, and the ten thousand things are allowed to enter and confirm us. The core, not just of our practice but of our lives, lies in releasing attachment to the concept of an internal separated "selfhood." If we get out of the way, forget ourselves by seeing the self so clearly it becomes porous, and let the ten thousand things claim us, we realize intimacy—another name for enlightenment.

Blake called our habitual attachment to the concept of an inner, separated selfhood "the limit of opaqueness" and named it stunningly, mischievously, and perhaps accurately "Satan." "Truly my Satan," he wrote, "you are a dunce." For Blake, Satan is our dunce-like tendency to *not* see beyond self-centeredness. Tangled up in thoughts of ourselves, we're unable to realize our deeper potential and more selfless nature. Yet the best moments of our lives are rarely those when we're caught up in self-concern. Instead, they tend to be those times when we forget ourselves, and the stars, a child, a river, or birdsong walk in. Still, self-concern is such a habit that, like addicts, we return to it again and again. And so we must choose to practice again and again, entering this moment as it is, ordinary, unfathomable, and never to be repeated.

Thinking that the arising of thought and feeling is a permanent "self," we become isolated, cut off, and fearful. Yet, isolated as we are, stars still shine, the moon still swims across the night sky, and a golden sun still rises over green hills. For whom do these wonders take place? Not only do we often fail to see and appreciate them, we fail to grasp that stars, moon, clouds, sun, hills just as they are, are us. Nothing is separate, yet at the same time, each is fully itself. We suffer because of error and lack of application.

Lost in a robber-ridden, dark forest dream, we hunger for riches, fame, and power as bulwarks against aging, death, and the inconsequence of our own ordinary, unheralded, too-brief lives. We bend ourselves out of shape to ally ourselves with what seems to offer protection and permanence no matter the pain it might cause. This legacy of unresolved childhood conditioning turns us into sleepwalkers, blindly destroying oceans, forests, rivers, air, and fertile land.

Our task is to wake up, but because we fall asleep again and again, we must catch ourselves again and again, consciously choosing to practice awakening over and over. This practice of awakeness awakening continues endlessly. Even breath counting in meditation is not simply a practice of counting breaths. It is a practice of awakening to *this* breath, *this* count.

This is what we've signed on for. This is our life task, to find the self that runs the caravan. Dharma practice asks us to look, really look. It makes sense. If we want to wake up, we must look into the root of sleep. Looking into this fully, deeply, and intimately ultimately means the realization of our own mind, yours and mine.

Yet even the Buddha wasn't always on the high road. We have this odd little past-life jataka where he's a robber. Even so, he's the kind of person we can't help but like—the rogue-as-hero, a Han Solo type—who, while seemingly only out for himself, remains ready to put himself at risk for others and the right. This is a character type with strength, freedom, and a readiness to take risks and accept consequences: in short, with life energy. Labels can be deceptive. To the Sheriff of Nottingham, Robin Hood was a very bad man.

Buddhist practice doesn't ask us to get rid of ourselves or to become another, better, more spiritual self. Rather, we are asked to realize the self that already is us to the bottom, just as we are. The point is not to free us to do what we want, when we want. It's not to make us a better *this* or *that*, or better *at* this or that. The aim is to free us from ourselves, from the self we cherish, the self we may lie, cheat, steal, even kill to protect; from our obsessive, habitual, compulsive, anxiously cramped interest in ourselves, in who we think we are, and what we think or have been taught to think we want. This practice is not about contemplating navels. It is about releasing not just navels but eyes, ears, noses, tongues, bodies, minds. It is about realizing the freedom that has been ours from the start. It is about seeing the so-called ten thousand things as they are, intimately, truly.

Like the young man in the jataka, without the clarity of ongoing practice-realization, we can read the signs totally wrong. The person who tells us what we don't want to hear becomes an enemy. The person who tells us what's pleasing becomes a friend. Yet the rainy day that ruins our picnic can lead to unforeseen good, and the too easy, smooth path can slide us into ruin. Tossed about by circumstances, like the young man in the jataka we put ourselves in harm's way through ignorance of who and what we, and all things, are. So we stumble about, fouling our nest, burning down the house we're still living in.

The Bodhisattva as a robber remains on the Great Way. Karma has brought him to his robber employment. He seems to be the opposite of what he was in the jataka where he risked his life to protect others *from* robbers. Robbers violate Buddhist precepts, the second of which is resolving not to take what is not given but to respect the things of others. Robbery, then, would be out. You'd think a bodhisattva would know that! Yet is the Bodhisattva necessarily less a bodhisattva as a robber and more of a bodhisattva as a protector from robbers? To answer we'd have to know his motivation, what the times and karma demanded, what the local government was up to, what the wealthy community was doing. After all, we often like the rule-breaker with a good heart better than the self-righteous prig who can easily turn into a bully.

Corporations steal land from peasants who, protesting to preserve their homes, are called "thieves" by corporate-controlled media. Which side better upholds the precepts?

Or how about the first Buddhist precept: "I resolve not to kill but to cherish all life"? What about killing as a way to prevent more killing? To kill, not out of vengeance or punishment, but to protect others and prevent more harm could express a high and selfless ideal. What about killing a murderer, let's say a Hitler, not just to stop him from harming others, but to keep him from murdering his own deepest potential and causing himself even greater karmic harm? Would this, too, be murder or an act of compassion?

And here's the Bodhisattva, a thief in a past life. It's been said that Zen teachers are thieves, stealing away our long-cherished beliefs, hard-gripped truths, self-righteous treasures, and blind adherence to unexamined points of view. Our practice opens doors, unlocks windows, and lets the robber of realization break in to steal us blind. When everything we thought we were is gone, what may we then find? As the song says, "Freedom's just another word for nothing left to lose."

Maybe as the leader of a robber band the Bodhisattva was perfecting his skill, preparing for the moment lifetimes ahead when he would be teacher to all beings, working to rob his students of deeply seated, delusive, limiting preconceptions. Being a robber might turn out to be a useful skill for helping others. Or maybe he was doing good, taking money from those who'd stolen from poor farmers and honest tradesmen. Some laws are unethical. To be ethical we might have to break them. A man steals a loaf of bread to feed a starving child. A resistance fighter robs a

Nazi collaborator to save Allied fliers. The story does not give us contexts. Things might not be quite what a label like "robber" implies.

Even as a robber, the Bodhisattva had skill and power. He could "understand the language of animals"—a kind of universal ancient shorthand for indicating that someone has great wisdom. It means that self-centeredness has dropped away to such a degree that the cat, bird, or fox can be understood. It means you're so intimate with your own nature you're intimate with all. Such a person resides at the core of life—where no charlatan or egomaniac can abide.

So, while the Bodhisattva may be a robber, he is also a person of wisdom and compassion. He doesn't take the boy's money—not a penny! And he lets him go, taking some guff for it from his men, as well. Could a saint do better? Then, again, maybe he's a rogue but with good karma from his past. He saw this young man, grasped what was up, was moved, then did something that lost him money and caused his men to grumble but that nevertheless felt right and good, expressing something maybe even he couldn't name. His deep appreciation of a deeper ethic is revealed not by the wildness of his life, but by his willingness to restrain that wildness, and set aside the unconscious self-interest that to one degree or another drives us all.

No one is excluded from the Path. With all our shortcomings, flaws, and past bad choices we can, with Right Now practice, work to embody the Way, drop self-centeredness, and uphold the precepts of our deeper nature.

While we are not as gifted with awareness as the Bodhisattva-robber, by practicing regularly we, too, can begin to listen well, see clearly, decipher signs correctly, and do what's right.

This is our choice, our life's work, our growing determination, and deepest vow.

Sixteen

The Ogre Child: Finding the Way No Matter Who You Are

Padakusalamanava Jataka, No. 432

A queen lies to her husband about an affair, swearing that if she lied, may she become a *yaksha*—a man-eating ogress with a long face like a horse. She dies and is, indeed, reborn as a yaksha. Carrying a handsome Brahmin to her cave to eat, she remembers her human life. Then, instead of killing the Brahmin, she marries him and the two live together as man and wife. The Bodhisattva is born as their child.

The yaksha keeps her husband and son locked in her cave, blocked with a huge boulder. When still young, the Bodhisattva rolls the stone away and tells his mother that he and his father can't live in darkness. His ogress mother begins to worry that he will leave her. And indeed, in time the Bodhisattva decides to help his father return to his original, human home. He tries, but the ogress catches them. The Bodhisattva then asks about the size of his mother's domain—the land he will eventually inherit. Once he knows its limits, he tries again, carrying his father on his shoulders (he is a fast runner) to the river boundary of her territory.

When they're halfway across the river, his mother—who runs even faster—arrives and pleads with them to return. His father goes back to her, but the Bodhisattva refuses. His mother, seeing that her son is determined to make his way in the world, says that the world of men is treacherous. And she gives him a magical gift to help him do well there—tracking skills which will allow him to track footsteps even in the air and even if twelve years have passed since the steps were made. Then the yaksha, his mother, dies of a broken heart.

The Bodhisattva and his father perform her funeral rites then head for the city where the Bodhisattva is hired by the king as a tracker. A minister insists the king find out if the boy is as good as he claims. The minister and king steal jewels from the treasury and, making a complicated journey from the palace to the city's water tank below, hide them there. The Bodhisattva, commanded by the king to find the missing jewels and reveal the thieves, follows footsteps, even those appearing in the air, and finds the jewels. But he will not reveal the thieves. The king insists. The Bodhisattva tries to dissuade the king, telling pointed stories about the harm caused when things—or people—who we count on for protection let us down. Stupidly the king refuses to get the point, insisting that the Bodhisattva must reveal the thieves. Then the Bodhisattva tells all, exposing the king and minister. The people are outraged that their king and his minister, whom they trusted, were willing to create such turmoil, unnecessarily disrupting lives, and throwing the city into chaos. They are dismayed, too, that the king was too foolish to understand the Bodhisattva's message of harmony, trust, and decorum. They then kick out the king and minister as unworthy leaders, and install the Bodhisattva, child of an ogre, on the throne instead.

———◊———

"Then the prophecies of the old songs have turned out to be true, after a fashion," said Bilbo.
"Of course," said Gandalf. "And why should they not prove true?"
—J.R.R. Tolkien

Every day we hear stories, tell stories, and tell ourselves stories. Buddhism is a story, as is the self, rehearsing its narrative through the days and events of our lives. Our path of inquiry means waking to the nature of the elusive narrator and, then, doing the work needed to shift the narrative. "Do good, avoid evil, save the many beings"—the so-called "Three Resolutions"—is the path of all buddhas. This is the story we work on telling daily with action and with practice, not simply with words.

Stories set expectations and have consequences. The jatakas don't always show the Bodhisattva as a perfect being. Often he's a work in progress, making mistakes, struggling to do the right thing. As fanciful as jatakas can be with their talking animals, devas, yakshas, nagas, and kinnaras, such straight talk gives us room to consider that, odd as they are, they might be truer than we think. They are not mere hagiographies, but show the Buddha-to-be as an unfinished product, warts and all.

Here the Bodhisattva is born into less than ideal circumstances. That's an understatement: he's the child of an ogress who eats human flesh, and he and his father are locked in a cave to keep them from running off and getting away! That's a pretty hard start in life, to be literally caught in a confining, potentially devouring love. Even worse, the Bodhisattva in this past life is only half-human; his other half is primitive, elemental, earthy, monstrous. Yet, despite this, he is honest, skillful, determined, and kind. He helps his father, performs rites for his mother, and tries to keep a king from ruin.

We fall into traps when we start comparing stories. "Am I good enough? Do I have what it takes?" are self-limiting tales. We have this breath, this brief moment in which to choose to act on our vow to awaken and be of use to all. It is a choice we make again and again. If we don't, we fall back into the cave of our old story and end up treading the small bit of real estate we've inherited. Roshi Kapleau used to say, "We each had a mother and a father. It's enough." In other words, having been born gives us the opportunity to begin doing the work. Zen Buddhism affirms that our nature right now is none other than the nature of Buddha. The Bodhisattva's nature, even as the child of an ogress, was no different than his nature as Shakyamuni Buddha. He doesn't acquire a different, better nature later on. His nature and our nature, the Dharma affirms, are no different from fundamental or original nature, the originating principle of all buddhas and bodhisattvas. "From the beginning all beings are Buddha," says Zen master Hakuin's "Song in Praise of Zazen." *All beings*—not just those with good cheekbones, above average intelligence, and supportive life circumstances. Hakuin's song ends, "This very body, the body of Buddha." This flawed, aging, somewhat ogreish body, *this* very body, he says, is Buddha. What does this mean?

Maybe your mother was an ogress, or your father an ogre. Maybe you are a bit ogreish yourself, showing the effects of your ogre lineage, ogreish upbringing, ogreish meals and vacations as well as, perhaps, having been locked in a cave by an ogreish parent, deprived of the light and air you craved. Your ogreish past created complexities and difficulties you deal with today. Join the club.

The Bodhisattva—the Buddha in a past life—was the same.

In this jataka he had a complex relationship with his mother and his father. His parents had quite different backgrounds. Could they even understand one another? They didn't sit down at the same table or share the same meals (most Brahmins don't eat meat, let alone humans!). And yet, there was something between them, as well as between them and their child. They were a family. Who can explain karma? Like the Bodhisattva, we, too, may discover that unpromising circumstances have given us enough fuel to light our Dharma fire.

Even an ogre can show love. Hard hearts can melt and blood-drinking, fanged, and frowning mouths turn up in tender smiles. The queen who'd become an ogress by living a lie found fulfillment and love as a parent! What was her karma with the Bodhisattva? What would their future karma be? Lifetimes in the future was she Queen Maya, the Buddha's birth mother, who died seven days after his birth? Or was she, perhaps, his maternal aunt, Prajapati, who took on the role of stepmother when his mother died? While the story doesn't reveal her future identity, some relationship was at work that might yet unfold in lives to come. As an ogress, she's almost sweetly human, pressuring her husband and son not to leave. What loving mother hasn't had such a wish? What parent?

And what of her magical gift? We've all received magical gifts from our ancestors, gifts of language, aptitude, and skills ranging from knowing how to tie our shoes, to a talent for playing piano or painting pictures. In this case the gift is exactly what her child will need. The vision of the tale is one of freedom and potential. With the right skills and attitude anything is possible. Even an ogress's child might become king.

The Buddhist view dramatized by the jatakas is clear: birth doesn't make us who we are. Practice, aspiration, and deeds make us who we are. Someone from the lowest level of ancient India's caste-bound society, upon entering the sangha, could equal or surpass the noblest. A barber entering the Order before a prince would be senior and held in higher regard.

The ogress mother gives her child a miraculous gift—the ability to track footsteps, even those in the air, and even if they'd been left twelve years back. Then, heartbroken, she dies. Awakening a tender heart, she is released from her ogress body. Her ogress karma, the result of a self-centered lie, is done. She finds freedom through love. Like her bodhisattva son, she does not let an ogress nature prevent her from experiencing something higher. Even as an ogress, she attained a condition of selfless love. Perhaps no condition is totally destructive; certainly none are permanent. A foolish vow from her previous, selfish life leads to transformation.

They say that sages can see tracks left by birds flying across the sky. Maybe animals can too. Andre, the seal, honorary harbormaster of Rockport, Maine, was brought to the Boston Aquarium by car to be kept safe through the harsh winter months. Come spring, Andre was taken to Boston Harbor and released. Four days later he showed up back in Rockport, having swum two hundred miles through a part of the sea he had never even seen before. Had he followed scent trails, star patterns, or . . . what? For him, there was a trail of footsteps he could follow. After that, that's how he got home every year, swimming on his own.

We also follow footsteps. Teaching stories, sutras, ceremonies, koans, Buddhas on altars are all signs, footprints left for us by those who've walked the Path before. There are billions of humans on this planet. Many don't see such signs. Somehow we, as Dharma students, do. Is this ability the gift of our parents? Of our karma? Love can be strange, coming to and from us in odd ways, not necessarily fairy-tale or happy-ending movie ways. No childhood is perfect. Not even the Buddha's. Prince Siddhartha's, "He Whose Wishes Are Fulfilled," mother died shortly after his birth. His father, worried about a prophecy that said if his son saw impermanence he'd give up the throne, kept constant watch over him. That constant, hovering parental anxiety must have marred what might have otherwise been a happy, even enviable childhood.

Following the Buddha's footsteps, we learn to uncover the wisdom in old teaching tales and begin to move the boulder that seals us in our familial cave. Outside what Blake called our "caverned self" is air, light, color, and life. Once we start practicing, we need not be overly concerned with any of the less-than-perfect aspects of our upbringing or inheritance. Of course, if there are problems that shut us down or stymie us, we should get the help we need to work on and with them. We mature by dealing with issues, not by ignoring or trying to push past what's on our plate.

Long ago the Buddha, in this past life as the child of an ogress, didn't let a difficult, less-than-perfect upbringing stop him. He used his gifts—intelligence, wisdom, sensitivity, and talent—to go as far as he could. Ogreish as we also are, the story points to our potential. The Path continues.

Let's keep going and see for ourselves what lies ahead.

Seventeen

Hairy Kassapa: Even Great Sages Make Mistakes

Lomakassapa Jataka, No. 433

The Bodhisattva, named Kassapa, is the son of the royal priest, and his best friend, Brahmadatta, is the prince and royal heir. When the king dies, Brahmadatta becomes king. Kassapa thinks: "He will offer me wealth and power. What need have I for such things? I choose to devote myself to the way of the sages." So off he goes into the Himalayas, dedicated to intense spiritual practice.

Shakra, king of the gods, grows concerned. The Bodhisattva, now named Lomakassapa or Hairy Kassapa because of his long hair and hairy body, is meditating so rigorously that Shakra thinks: "I must slow him down or in time he'll supplant me. I must make him slip up."

Late in the night the radiant god, Shakra, awakens Brahmadatta, king of Varanasi, and tells him he must have his old friend Lomakassapa perform a sacrifice of many animals. If he does, Shakra says, Brahmadatta will not only gain long life but will become king of all India. Overjoyed, Brahmadatta sends his most senior councilor to offer Lomakassapa a vast hermitage if he will return to Varanasi and perform the sacrifice. But the Bodhisattva refuses saying, "I'd never harm living beings."

Shakra reappears and discovering the failure, tells the king to try again. "But this time," he says, "offer him your beautiful daughter, Chandavati, in marriage. Lomakassapa has been alone for a long time and is a man." The councilor returns with Chandavati, the king's daughter, and again makes the request. Seeing the girl, this time the Bodhisattva agrees. In Varanasi, a great sacrificial pit has been dug and a long line of animals now waits beside it. The Bodhisattva is handed a great sword with which to do the killing. As he raises it to strike the first animal in the line, the crowd of people shouts, "Stop! You are a man of peace, and should not kill!"

The elephant that is about to be killed had previously seen service in the king's wars. When the sword is raised toward his neck, he recognizes his danger and trumpets loudly in terror. All the other animals also scream and bellow. The Bodhisattva hearing the shouts, screams, and bellows, remembers his vows. Ashamed, he lowers his weapon.

The king begs him to continue, but rising cross-legged in the air, Lomakassapa gives a Dharma talk on impermanence, attention, compassion, selflessness, and repentance then flies back to his hermitage.

————◊————

He with body waged a fight,
But body won; it walks upright.
—W.B. Yeats

In this jataka the Bodhisattva, already a sage far along the path of wisdom and compassion trips, stumbles, and almost falls—into a deep pit of error. Caught by a compelling delusion, it is only the voice of the people and of the terrified beasts that bring him back to himself in time.

There is something beast-like about this hairy sage. Covered in hair like an animal, he's caught by the primal realm of animal desire and instinct. No matter how refined our practice or how long we keep at it, we're still mammals with hair, glands, hormones, eyes, ears, and minds—and all that comes with them. Dharma practice, as this jataka shows, is never a habit; practice-realization never on automatic. Even good habits, like gold dust in the eye, can block our vision. Better than a good thing, an old Zen saying tell us, is nothing at all.

But "nothing" doesn't mean simply following a path of impulse and calling it "going with the flow." The Middle Way is not about staying in some imagined "middle ground" between extremes. It's about finding balance and harmony in all we do. Emptiness is form, form emptiness. These are not simply words in a chant, but the core of practice-realization. The precepts are not an add-on to a free Zen life. They *are* that life fully, consciously expressed. Ethics and emptiness are the Middle Way, and are one and the same.

So, realization of vast emptiness doesn't mean, "anything goes." Yet there remains that sticky thing called "desire." It can't be stopped or repressed, though cultures have tried; cults of castration litter history. But simply calling it "natural" and letting it run amok to ruin lives is no solution, either. Neither extreme of either denying it or giving it free rein will work. Where is the Middle Way? That is, how do we live well *with* it?

If you think this is a theoretical question, you're not paying attention. We all have to come to terms with this and we all can fall, even the Bodhisattva. There are at least several jatakas that dramatize his struggle with sexual desire. In some, as with this one, he almost falls. In at least one he *does* fall and has to repent, change his ways, and start over again.

And, while in this jataka his answer to the challenge involves returning to a dedicated, solitary, mountaintop sort of life, in other jatakas he is married and has a family. Celibacy is not the point; vows, truthfulness, and intention are.

Desire need not only be about sex (though Freud might disagree). It could be desire for anything that makes our knees weak, hearts race, and palms sweaty—even spiritual experiences! Desire is a force we all reckon with, so ever-present that advertising can make us drool over things we hardly need. Without ethical teachings at the core of our practice, even the desire for enlightenment can become poison.

Compared to the full maturity of Buddhahood, everyone is a child with much growing up yet to do—perhaps we've already seen the painful effects of our immaturity. Knowing our own potential for error is what makes our Dharma practice real. We're not trying to *look like* Buddhists or buddhas. We're not on an enlightenment safari, searching for that spiritual buzz to check off our list before rushing on to the next sexy thing. We are practicing because, like the Buddha, we've seen consequences. We've held our thoughts and actions up to the light of our vows and learned that we need to mature. We know that we can do more and can do better.

All it takes (ha!) is that we drop our ingrained, upside-down, topsy-turvy, habitual, dualistic self-centeredness and get out of the way. The Dharma offers practice, not theory. And it reminds us that if we persist through challenges, issues, and errors, then like the Bodhisattva we *will* mature. Growing up looks exactly like what this jataka shows it to be: making mistakes, falling down, getting back up, correcting errors, continuing on.

Consider the act of walking: We lift a foot, fall forward, and catch ourselves as our foot touches ground. We lift the other foot, fall, and catch ourselves. We do this over and over. Walking is falling and catching, falling and catching. Eventually we get so good at it we no longer notice that moving forward means falling. This is a good description of the Path.

The Buddha, the narrator of each jataka, was humble enough in telling his own past-life tales to not shy away from revealing his difficulties. As most of us try to hide our shortcomings, we can be especially grateful for such honesty.

The king in this jataka makes the same self-centered mistake as the Bodhisattva-ascetic. He's willing to manipulate an old friend, give away his daughter, and slaughter living beings to get what he wants. Though he may attempt to whitewash his actions by claiming he only wants power to do good things, starting his reign like this casts doubt on his ability to pull it off. Shakra, too, though the highest god, seems motivated by petty concerns. But, after all, all beings within the six realms of unenlightened existence (even the heavens and god realms) have some issue, some self-centeredness that keeps the karmic wheel turning. At least once in the jatakas, the Bodhisattva himself ruled as Shakra, king of the gods. In another he ruled alongside many Shakras. Yet high as he was, he, too, was caught by self-centeredness and fell. But, because of his error, he saw the effects of his own narrow thoughts and behaviors and was forever positively changed.

In this jataka we see that even someone far along the Path can fall. The wheel turns. King of the gods, human king, realized ascetic, all are put to the test. But there is one difference. Through years of ongoing practice the hermit-sage retains access to living vows. Though they're clouded, they're there. This changes things not only for himself but for the animals, the king, and even, perhaps, for the king of the gods. Avoid evil, do good, save the many beings. The Bodhisattva catches himself just in time, achieving the Middle Way even as he teeters at the edge of the pit. Still, it's touch-and-go until the crowd speaks up.

Which is an important point. Our practice is not a way of shutting out the world. As often as circumstances challenge and test us, they can also help us actualize the Way. The ascetic was drawn from his mountaintop through desire, a seeming stumble on his path. But perhaps the news was not all bad. Perhaps he was freed of pride and freed, too, of the false sense of superiority that can come from an isolated, untested practice. Maybe Shakra had something up his godly sleeve, after all. The gods, we are told, move in mysterious ways. He set the game in motion. The upshot was that the Bodhisattva was freed from a narrow, one-sided realization.

Perhaps that was Shakra's intent all along. Under the guise of selfish motivation, in stealth mode he stepped in and changed the story. Sometimes problems, slips, and challenges can save us from a too settled, complacent practice or life. The Bodhisattva almost fell into disaster and was saved, called back to his deepest vows by animals and ordinary folk. Perhaps he was not so special after all. Maybe his failure was a good thing, freeing him to become more conscious and more alert. Swelled heads have a way of hitting the doorframe when we try to walk through.

The Buddha-Just-About-To-Be sat beneath the bodhi tree through a long, challenging night of meditation. With the dawn he glanced up and saw the morning star. Maybe it was a slip in concentration. But with that little error, that marvelous *failure*, the universe stepped in and the rest is, literally, history. After that came all the comings and goings back in the world. Sometimes what look like mistakes can be Dharma gates.

Let's not get complacent, content with a comfortable, one-sided, fuzzy sort of abstract practice. Remaining open to *specifics*, to this morning star, this friend, this flower, this breath, as well as to our own lapses and shortcomings, like the Bodhisattva we can do our best to turn difficulties and failures into the Path, finding ways to turn our straw into gold.

Eighteen

Touching the Earth

Nidana-Katha (introduction to the Pali Jataka collection—and elsewhere)

When Prince Siddhartha Gautama is twenty-nine, for the first time he truly sees aging, sickness, and death and catches a glimpse of the spiritual path that leads beyond anguish. Soon after, he leaves his palace, enters the forests and mountains to begin his search for truth, and never looks back. After six years of horrific austerities, near death, a skeleton wound around with sinews and veins, he suddenly remembers a festival from his childhood when self-consciousness had fallen away and he'd experienced deep selfless absorption and profound peace.

He realizes if he'd already glimpsed the Way as a well-fed child, then starvation and punishment of the body can't be the Path. He accepts food—a simple offering of milk rice. His five ascetic disciples leave him in disgust at what they take to be this sign of his having given up. But he hasn't.

After eating he tosses his empty bowl onto the river: "If this is the day of my supreme enlightenment, may it float upstream!" The bowl forges upstream, then whirls down into the chambers of the ancient naga king, Kala Nagaraja, coming to rest against a long row of identical bowls—the bowls of previous Buddhas. Arriving at the bodhi tree, he announces, "Though only skin, sinews, and bones remain and my blood and flesh dry up and wither away, I won't leave this spot until I've attained full enlightenment."

Visions arise. The three beautiful daughters of Mara the Tempter, Mara the Distractor, try to seduce him. Mara's terrifying demonic army whirls down upon him. He remains fully focused and unmoved. Then Mara approaches and in Gautama's own internal voice, asks: "How could you, young as you are, be worthy of coming to supreme enlightenment? You couldn't be ready."

The future Buddha touches the Earth, asking the Earth to witness for him. The Earth replies, "He is worthy! There is not a spot where he has not already offered himself to the attainment of enlightenment and the welfare of all!"

Mara and his hosts flee.

With the dawn, the Buddha glances at the morning star and finds enlightenment, exclaiming, "Wonder of wonders! All beings are buddhas, fully endowed with wisdom and virtue! Only delusion prevents them from attesting to it."

―――――◊―――――

The melons look cool,
Flecked with mud
From the morning dew.
　　　　―Basho

This story of the Buddha's enlightenment is not itself a jataka, but it is Buddhism's archetypically central tale. It is where all the jatakas lead.

Enlightenment is both the goal and the daily beating heart of Zen practice-realization—and it goes beyond mere *calm*.

For Siddhartha, calm wasn't enough. Having personally experienced impermanence, the insubstantiality of every person and thing, a fire was lit in his mind, heart, and gut. After that he had no choice. He had to keep going until he touched solid ground.

Wherever we are, whatever we may have realized or *not* realized, we can take this to heart and also keep going. We do the work. Then we keep doing the work. We may have moments in which we touch the ground of Mind but these are not the end of our road. Rather they are a new beginning, like realizing, "Aha! Here's the ground!" We can then continue our journey with greater confidence, sure now that real ground is under our feet.

In many jatakas the Bodhisattva wakes to the reality of selflessness, the identity of form and emptiness, of relative and absolute, to nondual True Nature—to insight. These are milestone moments to be sure, but not yet full realization of original buddhahood. In past jataka lives, Prince Siddhartha had been a spiritual teacher, lay practitioner, ordained practitioner, hermit-monk, community leader, wandering ascetic, businessman, family man, carpenter, juggler, robber, ox herder, farmer, caravan leader—to say nothing of animals, gods, ogres, and nagas. The list seems almost endless.

He had countless lives committed to basic ethical practices whether as a human or nonhuman being. Buddhist tradition says whatever challenges he faced, whatever heights he reached or depths he sounded, he always chose to go further, over the next hill, beyond the next river, through the next dark forest. Not ignoring a problem, not satisfied with a milestone, he actualized the Great Way. Onward, further, was his nature, as it is our own. Practice-realization is not static, but a dynamic road continuing endlessly—and thus it is called the Path, the Way.

But we especially revere the story of the Buddha's enlightenment because it reveals our potential even as it shows the work, the perseverance and dedication necessary to achieve it. The Buddha has his Christ-on-the-Cross moment when he discovers that willful asceticism hasn't clarified a thing, only left him in a dark, useless place. And though the ex-prince sat and sat, in the end, just sitting wasn't enough either; there was a trigger to his realization. It didn't just come from looking "within." It could have been a word, a sound, or anything. He was ripe, his mind empty of habitual limits, when he glanced up and saw the morning star. *AHA!* "Gone, gone, entirely gone!" Completely clear! A morning star sat beneath the tree. No seeing is real seeing. No one sitting is genuine sitting. Just star! *Star!*

But even before that, the Bodhisattva wasn't just sitting there like a frog. He was poised, alert as a cat before a mouse hole. When Mara challenged, he responded. He didn't get caught up, but he didn't ignore it. When situations arise in our lives, we can't go off and sit until they're gone. There is a time to act. It need not be a big deal. In fact, it would be wise not to make it—whatever it is—a big deal. The Buddha simply touched the Earth and asked the Earth to witness for him. He didn't try to muster reasons and out-argue Mara. He simply did the one small thing that would do the job.

Mara was no slouch and knew how to hit a nerve. Perhaps self-doubt is what all obstacles come down to. One old teacher said that if it wasn't for some form of not giving ourselves fully to the inquiry, some form of holding back and doubting in a not useful way, we'd all have been enlightened ages ago. The doubting voice of Mara is ancient and universal, but need not be an obstacle. It's simply another Dharma gate we vow to wake to. We're all in the same boat. The Buddha was no different.

Buddhist tradition says that we all have the nature of Buddha, exactly the same vast empty nature of endlessly creative potential. From the first we are fully endowed with wisdom and compassion. And because it is already who we are, *if* we practice, *if* we make the effort, then we, too, can to one degree or another awaken to Original Mind.

But again, let's be clear: enlightenment is not a "thing" we "get." It comes from losing not gaining, losing the habitual self-centered "stuff" that cuts us off from wind, rain, sun, moon, stars, animals, people. With that wonderful failure, that liberating loss, we find intimacy, which is what we've been seeking for who knows how long. *Enlightenment* is a name given to our being able to attest to our original, unblemished intimacy with everything sentient and nonsentient. It's not a prize. We do not gain it, because it has never been lost. Like the ground, it has always been here. We just didn't quite have the steadiness to see it. Of course, it's not that "I" become intimate with everything. Rather the so-called "ten thousand things" step in and replace me. I'm gone. Intimacy is that intimate!

At some point we begin to think, "If we are this enlightened nature, where is it? And why don't we know it?" In our ongoing meditation we bore into such questions like a thirsty person drilling for water. A sonar survey—the life of the Buddha, the jatakas, Zen teaching—shows us that water is there. We have a map. Our map reveals that all the water we'll need is already beneath our feet. So we keep at it. We enter a sangha. We sit in silence with others. We hear Dharma talks, meet and work with teachers, and make time for retreats—we experience each breath, explore and personalize specific teachings, examine and uphold precepts. If we are Zen students we may work on koans.

The Buddha, an ex-prince, touched the Earth after lifetimes of practice. For many people, it is not until years of practice and various initial milestones have gone by that the Gate really opens and they *know*. Still, the Buddha's enlightenment, tradition holds, was unique. It was complete, unsurpassed, and perfect—every level of character and mind fully realized. And it was so because of the lifetimes of work that preceded it.

In substance, each experience of realization, both the small kind we're likely to realize and the Buddha's own great enlightenment, is the same. But in content they are vastly different. Buddhist mythos says that in this world age no one experienced more deeply than Shakyamuni because no one had worked so hard or so long to prepare the ground. He touched not only the ground but the bottomless bottom and topless heights. Comparing our realization to his would be like comparing the finger painting of a kindergartner to the finished work of a Rembrandt or Picasso. The substance is the same—both are paintings—but the degree of conscious realization is vastly different. Yet we all begin somewhere, and for the kindergartner that finger painting is as meaningful as Rembrandt's work was for him.

The Buddha's story—his home-leaving and forest-path exertions, his abandonment by his disciples and his solitary encounter with Mara, the primordial force of his and our innate ignorance—completes his path of many lifetimes. Touching the Earth, he gets up and walks on, transcending the final temptation to sit at ease in his long-sought, hard-won pavilion of enjoyment, freedom, wisdom, and peace. Instead, he devotes his next fifty years to walking the dusty roads, teaching those who, while in reality as complete and whole as he, don't know it. He goes back into the chaos of the ten thousand things, at peace with it all, a half-smile on his lips.

Just prior to the Buddha's enlightenment, after six years of exhaustive effort (to say nothing of kalpas of jataka practice-exertions), going the limit, trying with all he had, drawing on the power of his own efforts, failures, and triumphs, Mara, the inner voice of ego, appears. And Mara draws his ace in the hole—self-doubt. He asks, "How could a sheltered ex-prince like you be worthy of the goal? Better men and women than you have tried and failed. You're young, just a beginner. Give it time. You've got some basic ability, but now? No way. Back off! Take it slow." Mara's advice is reasonable, devilishly reasonable. "Take it easy. Be careful. Go slow. Prepare. Reduce attachments and ego concerns. Be humble. Don't be hasty."

At this crucial juncture, with worlds in the balance, Siddhartha doesn't waste breath arguing with the habit voice of his own separateness, his predilection toward egotism. He doesn't even try to put together a reasonable counterargument. To enter the fray is to have already lost. "Ready? Not ready? A self that gains? A self that loses? A self that has *it*? A self that doesn't?" He doesn't get sucked into Mara's metaphor at all. Maybe he smiled and shook his head in pity for old Mara, then reached down and touched the humble Earth, asking her to be his witness. The Earth replied with thousands of voices—voices of furrows and graves, youth and age, man, woman, child, animals, plants, rivers, and stones. "Interbeing," to use Thich Nhat Hanh's lovely term, awakes, and Mara is overwhelmed. His last effort to tempt the Bodhisattva to cling to a limited view is crushed.

Jataka tales are the record of the Buddha's practice history. It is said to be a long history going back world ages, maybe Big Bangs. According to Buddhist tradition we, too, have our own jataka history. Things happened that made us who we are. We stumbled, scratched our knees, got up, let the wound scab, and tried again. We met joys and sorrows. Perhaps our history extends back through ages as well. Where does the path of causation that unfolds as each plant, bug, animal, bird, us begin?

At his moment of final challenge the Buddha touched the Earth. He didn't reach toward the sky and beg for help from above. He didn't fall for Mara's metaphor, try to win the debate, and out-argue the Distracter. He touched the always present, selfless, sat-on, trod-on ground, and asked the Earth to speak for him. Her response confirms him and overwhelms all doubt. What builds solid ground beneath us is the work we do now. Roshi Kapleau used to say, "If you don't let the Dharma down, the Dharma will never let you down." No effort is wasted.

What makes it such a lovely story is that it's not simply ancient history. It's our story, too. This moment is part of the ongoing jataka series of the un-fully-realized buddhas we each are. Essential nature, Mind itself, the ground beneath us, is always here. Past lives, past thoughts, decisions, and events led to this present one in which we sit, walk, stand, speak, eat, work, worry, create, pick our noses. Come day's end, we say "good night," and lie down on the ground of our nature, the ground we practice from and have always been standing on whether we know it or not. This ground is always ready to testify if we ask.

Our fundamental vow as human beings is to know ourselves, to know who or what we are. Ordinary things confirm us, tell us, indeed, *make* us who we are every day. There is no barrier between us, and a single thing. Enlightenment is intimacy.

Touching the Earth is always possible because real ground is never far away.

Appendix: A Dream within a Dream—a Zen View

Yang-shan dreamed he went to Maitreya's realm and was led to the third seat. A senior monk struck the stand with a gavel and announced, "Today the monk in the third seat will preach."

Yang-shan rose, struck the stand with the gavel, and said, "The Dharma of the Mahayana is beyond the Four Propositions and transcends the Hundred Negations. Listen, listen."

—*Gateless Barrier*, Case No. 25

The Zen teacher, Yang-shan, dreams he's with the future Buddha, Maitreya, and that he's seated in a place of honor. Maitreya is said to be in the Tushita Heavens working right now on the skillful means (*upaya*) to help free deluded beings—i.e., us. He's expected to be back down here with us on Earth soon—within the next billion years or so. (Heavenly time is different than earthly. A few years there could be millions here.) Meanwhile, given his loving-kindness, it's said that he's already wandering our dusty highways and markets as a potbellied, shaven-headed, big-eared monk, giving candy to children to keep them from crying, trying to keep things on track with a smile, a word, a laugh, some toasted buns or chewy rice cakes. He's called Hotei in that form, and appears as our own fully realized nature in the tenth and final Zen ox-herding picture, dust covered, grinning broadly in the busy marketplace of life. (The twelfth-century ox-herding pictures lay out the entire Path of practice-realization.) You might see him in a Chinese restaurant. That round-bellied good luck "Buddha" is a populist image of something that's actually quite mysterious and profound.

Maitreya, the future Buddha, is working hard, hoping to do what Shakyamuni couldn't: liberate all of us still-deluded beings. And there's Yang-shan included in that lofty company, in the primo third seat, next to the Buddha and Maitreya. Suddenly he's handed the teacher's gavel and told, "Before this enlightened assembly including the Buddha and future Buddha, the best of the best, show your stuff!"

Picture something like that in your life. Before you, row upon row, sit the most high-ranking audience, the best of the best in your field, with maybe millions more watching on TV. Unexpectedly a gavel is put in your hands and you're asked to stand up and do your stuff! *Gulp!* In an instant radiant heaven becomes sweaty-palm nervous-land. But Yang-shan rises, strikes the gavel—*Whack!*—and presents his view: "The Dharma of the Mahayana is beyond the Four Propositions and transcends the Hundred Negations. Listen, listen." End of *teisho* (Dharma talk).

Not only is he in a dream, but he's using dream words, creating a dream within the dream. What is "beyond" all phrases, all words? What is it to "transcend" all philosophical positions? Is he saying that words and letters only point to truth, but can't reach it or bring us to it? That we must let go, transcend, and go beyond them to know truth, for *it*'s beyond all that?

Zen master Dogen might disagree. Words are truth themselves in his view, as much as stars and cats, crows and clouds. And what about values? Should we be beyond them, too? Is that what he means? What *does* Yang-shan mean when he says that we have to get *beyond* all philosophical positions, all words and phrases to realize the Dharma, the truth? Does he mean we should get rid of everything and jump into metaphysical mayonnaise?

And why did Wu-men (compiler of the *Gateless Barrier*) think this would be significant? It's a story of someone dreaming he said something in a dream! We don't want dreams, do we? We want truth! Isn't that why we practice? To wake up! We've had enough dreams. We want to awake! What's Wu-men, compiler of the early thirteenth-century *Gateless Barrier* collection of koan cases, commentaries, and verses up to?

Then, again, what could be more beyond all logic, reason, concepts, or positions than a dream within a dream? The old Celtic storytellers used a device known as "interlacement." They'd start a story, then tell a story in that story, and then tell another story in that story, and on and on, story within story within story, like Russian nesting dolls, until our ability to follow what's dream and what's real is gone. All we know, all we can know, is this moment. We're deep in a dream—maybe deeper than ever—and at the same time more present than ever, all concepts fallen away.

In Zen, dream-like events are termed *makyo*, meaning "mysterious, uncanny, strange, or delusive mind-states." Ultimately anything not enlightenment is makyo, a dream. From that perspective even our waking life is a makyo of sorts. In this life there are also low-level makyo as the mind quiets and long-buried images, ideas, and sensations bubble up. After a few days of sesshin, detailed movies can appear on the wall before us or in the grain of the wood on the floor. Or the walls or floor might seem to ripple. We're encouraged to let them come and go like images in a dream, not fixate on them or get involved, but continue with our practice. They are not the point; they are simply signs that things are warming up. When we're really cooking, they're gone. So we pay attention to our practice, counting breath, experiencing breath, sitting fully focused, thinking "not-thinking," or absorbing our attention in a koan.

But this dream of Yang-shan's is different. It is mysterious, permeated with meaning. When we wake from such a dream, we might smell the tang of incense on the air. Was it real? Was it a dream? Chuang Tzu, the Chinese philosopher/sage, had a dream in which he was a butterfly.

When he awoke he wondered, was he a man dreaming he was a butterfly, or a butterfly dreaming he was a man?

Some makyo can have deep significance and presage a deeper level of practice. A dream voice might offer real insight. A scientist might find the solution to a vexing problem, like Francis Crick seeing the coiling shape of DNA in a dream. A writer might find the solution to his novel-in-process, a musician hear the closing strains of the symphony she's yet to write. A Zen student might rise through a dream into wakefulness, all doubts fallen away. Artists, scientists, and religious practitioners know the power of dreams. Creativity may depend on it. We may call it vision or imagination, instinct or intuition, but there are clearly subtle realms like gifts, like grace. Maybe animals know it, too. What, after all, *is* instinct?

It's said that when Yang-shan woke from this dream and related it, his teacher Kuei-shan said, "You have attained the rank of sage." But that's not the point. Wu-men's commentary goes: "Tell me, did Yang-shan preach or not? If you open your mouth you are lost. If you shut your mouth you also miss 'it.' If you neither open your mouth nor keep it closed, you are one hundred and eight thousand miles off." One hundred and eight thousand is a Buddhist reference to the hundred and eight defilements that, with enlightenment, become the hundred and eight perfections or virtues. Still, if you open your mouth and say, "He did preach," you're lost. I mean, come on! It was a dream! He didn't say a thing. None of it happened! So how could he have preached? He dreamed it! If you dream you wrote a novel, did you write it? Well, perhaps, in another world, who knows?

Then, again, if you stay silent, you've missed it, too. For something did happen. If not, there would be no story. That's the truth. He preached profound words in a splendid dream. That's a fact. How can you not respond? Are you going to ignore facts—the things that happen—in order to have quiet and peace? If so, how real will your peace be? What kind of life would that be? Yang-shan really *did* have a dream in which he spoke in Maitreya's palace. But where is our freedom if saying yes is wrong, and if silence, too, is wrong? How are we free and how can we actualize that freedom if neither a positive nor negative stance will do? What does it mean that the truth of the Mahayana is *beyond* every concept, every philosophical position? What is it to be awake? What is it to be asleep? What is a dream and what is real? Here's our life in a nutshell. Are we real? Are we dreaming? Is it the one or the other? Or neither? How shall we respond? How *do* we respond?

There are self-centered dreams that plague us. "I want this so bad I'll do anything to get it." Fierce ambitions find their fuel here. Less drastic versions abound, forming the texture of ordinary, dualistic reality. "I'm in here, she's out there. That's a tree. That's a raindrop. That's a cow." Ordinary reality is a kind of commonly agreed-upon dream. "We are such stuff as dreams are made on," says Prospero, magician and stage manager of Shakespeare's *The Tempest*. True enough. Then there are odd, mixed-up rootless dreams, dreams of the night, the result, as old Scrooge says in *A Christmas Carol*, of the undigested pudding we ate too late at night.

And there are large, noble dreams, like the dream of Buddhist practice and of wanting, indeed, *vowing* to save all beings even while we're lost in dreams ourselves. That's a big dream, a wild, crazy, magnificent dream. This is the dream that Zen would have us dream, not just becoming calm, not just gaining some peace of mind, not just being "in the zone." Zen asks us to achieve the realization of the impossible dream of dropping self-centeredness and liberating all beings. A big dream, indeed!

My old teacher, Roshi Kapleau, used to say that enlightenment is a dream. It's our own Mind we're talking about. It's been ours from the start. What are we going to get with enlightenment that we don't already have? The problem is that we don't know it. So it's an important dream, this dream of enlightenment, a dream on which a great deal of good might depend. Without it and the efforts we make toward its realization, we live half-lives. We get up in the morning but hardly notice the miraculously rising sun, or the light on leaves at midday, or the moon and stars at night. We live in thoughts about things, not in things themselves. Ordinary mysteries abound. Yet while lost in the dream we live, we shouldn't discount the dream's worth. Like Yang-shan's dream talk, there is truth in dream actions and words. "Life is but a dream," the old song says. Laurens van der Post, in his book *The Heart of the Hunter*, goes further, relating a Bushman saying: "There is a dream dreaming us."

For a dozen years I was invited to tell stories at Zuni Pueblo, one of the most traditional Native communities of North America. Once as my wife, Rose, and I were driving out of Zuni, we saw a terrible figure striding down the highway—one of the fierce punisher kachinas, or sacred beings, a kind of wrathful form like you might find in Tibetan Buddhism. This particular kachina wore a big, sacred wooden mask with sharp teeth and bulging eyes and long black, bloody hair—bloody because one hand held a bloody knife (made of painted wood), and with that hand he's said to brush back his bangs, leaving them bloodstained. He would soon walk pass Dowa Yalanne Elementary School—the school that looks out on Dowa Yalanne—Sacred Corn Mountain. The teachers would run out and gather the children in before he got there. If they didn't, and those kids saw that terrifying punisher of wrongdoing, they would faint, dropping onto the asphalt of the schoolyard.

Myth isn't just something in a book by Joseph Campbell. Myth is real. Kachinas are real. Roshi Kapleau, who had a somewhat Rinzai-like personality, forceful and direct, took quite a Soto-like stance, intuitive and sensitive when it came to myth. He never spoke of Buddha "figures" or Buddha "statues." He always said, "the Buddha on the altar." Why? The Buddha is real. Maitreya is real. Yang-shan is real. You and I are real, too. Dogen wrote in "Painting of a Rice Cake," "If you say a painting is not real, then the myriad things are not real."

Then again, how real is "reality"? Isn't it in good part what we imagine it to be, or what we are conditioned to believe it to be? Aren't we ourselves in large part what we are conditioned to believe ourselves to be? Is reality "real," or is it, too, a kind of dream? "We *are* such stuff as dreams are made on." Bob Dylan adds in "Talkin' World War III Blues," "I'll let you be in my dream if I can be in yours." Dreams within dreams. Within a dream.

Shibayama Roshi in his commentary on this koan in *Zen Comments on the Mumonkan* mentions that, when the Japanese teacher Takuan was dying and was pressed by his disciples for a last verse, he picked up his brush and wrote a single word—*Dream*. Roshi Kapleau related that not long after he arrived at Hosshin-ji in Japan, a monk asked him, "Kapleau-*san*. Do you believe in dreams?" He said it took him many years of Zen practice before he grasped what that monk was getting at.

Do you believe in dreams? Who is it that believes in dreams? There is a dream dreaming dreams. There is a dream person teaching in a dream, to dream listeners in the koan, and right now to you in these words. Is that wrong? Is it wrong that our life is a dream? Does that belittle or demean a thing? It's not that it's "just a dream." Rather it's a *DREAM!* Do we need to change that? Do we need to make it more real? What would that look like? How different would it be? Think again of what Yang-shan said from his dream within a dream: "The Dharma of the Mahayana *is beyond* the Four Propositions, and *transcends* the Hundred Negations." Right now, not just one day in the future when we "get it," *right now* reality is beyond yes, no, up, down, dream, true, real, good, bad, wise, foolish. What is it then? Did Yang-shan express it fully? And how will we? For we must. Every day we, too, are in the third seat. Every day someone, some situation, some event puts a gavel in our hands and demands, "Speak words of truth!" But, "Speak! Speak!" might be the same as "Live! Live!" Or "Show! Show!"

Maybe Wu-men knew what he was doing in taking an old dream talk and pasting it on our foreheads like a miner's lamp. If we turn it on, the koan can illuminate our way. It's not just a story in a Buddhist book, any more than a kachina is just a figure in a book on myth or on native ethnography.

Now, here's Wu-men's verse:

In broad daylight under the blue sky,
He preached a dream in a dream.
Absurd! Absurd!
He deceived the entire assembly.

In broad daylight, under the vast blue sky where nothing can be hidden, no dream or shadow survive, he preached a dream in a dream. Wu-men says, "You've got to be kidding! He deceived them all! *That* was his big talk at this big moment in the assembly of past and future Buddhas!?"

Look again. What "them?" *Us!* He tricked *us!* And still is. Yang-shan may have played a trick, but so did Wu-men. They're both still at it, deceiving us now, tricking us out of our small, cramped dreams, our dreary, little, suffering-causing, alternately self-doubting/self-asserting nightmares, and pushing us out into the sunlight where for a moment we can blink our eyes and laugh. With this dream, Yang-shan and Wu-men have found a way to pull the wool not over, but *off* our eyes. And that's a pretty good trick, wouldn't you say?

The jatakas and all their human, animal, and nonhuman beings; all their talk of enlightenment, of gaining, losing, struggling, fulfilling, of buddhas, bodhisattvas, karma; of lifetimes, meditation, home-leaving, insight, hermitages, palaces, and practice halls are ultimately a *dream*. But unlike ordinary dreams, this dream is an alarm clock ringing at our bedside, rousing us to wake up and face the daylight of Right Now.

Bibliography

Aitken, Robert. *The Gateless Barrier.* San Francisco: North Point Press, 1991.
———. *The Mind of Clover: Essays in Zen Buddhist Ethics.* San Francisco: North Point Press, 1984.
———. *The Practice of Perfection: The Paramitas from a Zen Buddhist Perspective.* New York: Pantheon Books. 1994.
———. *Taking the Path of Zen.* San Francisco: North Point Press, 1982.
Arntzen, Sonja, trans. *Ikkyu and the Crazy Cloud Anthology: A Poet of Medieval Japan.* Tokyo: University of Tokyo Press, 1986.
Bloch, Chana, and Stephen Mitchell. *The Selected Poetry of Yehuda Amichai: Newly Revised and Expanded Edition.* Berkeley, CA: University of California Press, 1996.
Blyth, R.H., *Haiku: In Four Volumes.* Tokyo: Hokuseido Press, 1952–1974.
Cleary, Thomas, trans. *Book of Serenity.* Hudson, NY: Lindisfarne Press, 1990.
Cleary, Thomas and J.C., trans. *The Blue Cliff Record.* Boston: Shambhala Publications, 1992.
Cook, Francis Dojun, trans. *The Record of Transmitting the Light: Zen Master Keizan's Denkoroku.* Boston: Wisdom Publications, 2003.
Cowell, E.B., ed. *The Jataka, or Stories of the Buddha's Former Births.* Translated from the Pali. 3 vols. 1895. Reprint, London: Pali Text Society, 1973. Distributed by Motilal Banarsidass, Delhi.
de Saint-Exupery, Antoine. *Wind, Sand and Stars.* New York: Harcourt Brace, 1967.

Dresden, Mark J., trans. *The Jatakastava, or Praise of the Buddha's Former Births*. Vol. 45, part 5 of New Series. Philadelphia, PA: Transactions of the American Philosophical Society, 1955.

Erdman, David V., ed. *The Poetry and Prose of William Blake*. Garden City, NY: Doubleday & Company Inc., 1965.

Fitzgerald, Robert, trans. *Homer: The Odyssey*. Garden City, NY: Doubleday & Company, Inc., 1961.

Grimm, Brothers. *The Complete Grimm's Fairy Tales*. New York: Pantheon Books, 1972.

Hall, Donald. *Life Work*. Boston, MA: Beacon Press, 2003.

Herold, A. Ferdinand. Translated by Paul C. Blum. *The Life of the Buddha: According to the Legends of Ancient India*. Tokyo: Charles E. Tuttle Co., 1954.

Hinton, David, trans. *The Late Poems of Wang An-Shih*. New York: New Directions, 2015.

Hori, Victor Sogen. *Zen Sand: The Book of Capping Phrases for Koan Practice*. Honolulu: University of Hawaii Press, 2003.

Johnston, E.H., trans. *The Buddhacarita or Acts of the Buddha*. New Delhi: Oriental Books Reprint Corporation, 1972.

Kapleau, Philip. *The Three Pillars of Zen*. Revised and expanded edition. Garden City, NY: Doubleday, 1988.

Kipling, Rudyard. *The Jungle Book*. New York: Penguin Putnam Inc., 1987.

Koroche, Peter, trans. *Once the Buddha Was a Monkey: Aryasura's Jatakamala*. Chicago: The University of Chicago Press, 1989.

Martin, Rafe. *The Banyan Deer: A Parable of Courage and Compassion*. Somerville, MA: Wisdom Publications, 2010.

———. *Brave Little Parrot*. New York: G.P. Putnam's Sons, 1998.

———. *Endless Path: Awakening within the Buddhist Imagination; Jataka Tales, Zen Practice, and Daily Life*. Berkeley, CA: North Atlantic Books, 2010.

———. *Foolish Rabbit's Big Mistake*. New York: G.P. Putnam's Sons, 1985.

————. *The Hungry Tigress: Buddhist Myths, Legends, & Jataka Tales.* Completely revised & expanded edition. Cambridge, MA: Yellow Moon Press, 1999.

————. *The Monkey Bridge.* New York: Alfred A. Knopf, 1997.

Mitra, Rajendralal. *Sanskrit Buddhist Literature of Nepal.* Calcutta, India: Asiatic Society of Bengal, 1882.

Obeyesekere, Ranjini, trans. *Yasodhara, the Wife of the Bodhisattva: The Sinhala Yasodharavata (The Story of Yasodhara) and the Sinhala Yasodharapadanaya (The Sacred Biography of Yasodhara).* Albany, NY: State University of New York Press, 2009.

Oliver, Mary. *New and Selected Poems.* Boston: Beacon Press, 1992.

Poppe, Nicholas, trans. *The Twelve Deeds of the Buddha: A Mongolian Version of the Lalitavistara.* Seattle: University of Washington Press, 1967.

Pyle, Howard. *The Merry Adventures of Robin Hood.* New York: Dover Publications, 1968.

Rhys Davids, T.W., trans. *Buddhist Birth-Stories (Jataka Tales): The Commentorial Introduction Entitled Nidana-Katha; The Story of the Lineage.* London: George Routledge & Sons Ltd, n.d.

Rotman, Andy, trans. *Divine Stories: Divyavadana, Part 1.* Somerville, MA: Wisdom Publications, 2008.

Safina, Carl. *Beyond Words: What Animals Think and Feel.* New York: Henry Holt and Company, 2015.

Sasaki, Ruth Fuller, Iriya Yoshitaka, and Dana R. Fraser. *The Recorded Sayings of Layman P'ang: A Ninth-Century Zen Classic.* New York: Weatherhill, 1971.

Seaton, J.P., and Dennis Maloney. *A Drifting Boat: Chinese Zen Poetry.* Fredonia, NY: White Pine Press, 1982.

Shaw, Sarah, trans. *The Jatakas: Birth Stories of the Bodhisattva.* New York: The Penguin Group, 2006.

Shibayama, Zenkei. *Zen Comments on the Mumonkan.* New York: New American Library, 1974.

Snyder, Gary. *Mountains and Rivers without End.* Washington, DC: Counterpoint, 1996.

———. *The Practice of the Wild.* San Francisco: North Point Press, 1990.

———. *This Present Moment: New Poems.* Berkeley, CA: Counterpoint, 2015.

Stevens, John, trans. *One Robe, One Bowl: The Zen Poetry of Ryokan.* New York: Weatherhill, 1977.

———. *Rengetsu: Life and Poetry of Lotus Moon.* Brattleboro, VT: Echo Point Books & Media, 2014.

———. *Wild Ways: Zen Poems of Ikkyu.* Buffalo, NY: White Pine Press, 2003.

Stevens, Wallace. *The Collected Poems of Wallace Stevens.* New York: Alfred A. Knopf, 1991.

Tanahashi, Kazuaki, trans. *Treasury of the True Dharma Eye: Zen Master Dogen's Shobo Genzo.* Boston: Shambhala, 2010.

Tolkein, J.R.R. *The Hobbit.* Boston: Houghton Mifflin Company, 1966.

Trevor, M.H., trans. *The Ox and His Herdsman: A Chinese Zen Text with Commentary and Pointers by Master D.R. Otsu and Japanese Illustrations of the Fifteenth Century.* Tokyo: Hokuseido Press, 1969.

Un, Ko. *What?: 108 Zen Poems.* Berkeley, CA. Parallax Press, 2008.

Van der Post, Laurens. *The Heart of the Hunter: Customs and Myths of the African Bushman.* New York: Harcourt Brace Jovanovich, 1980.

Waddell, Norman, trans. *Poison Blossoms from a Thicket of Thorn: Hakuin Zenji.* Berkeley, CA: Counterpoint, 2014.

Watson, Burton, trans. *The Vimalakirti Sutra.* New York: Columbia University Press. 1997.

Wray, Elizabeth, Carla Rosenfeld, Dorothy Bailey, and Joe Wray. *Ten Lives of the Buddha: Siamese Temple Paintings and Jataka Tales.* New York: Weatherhill, 1972.

Yeats, William Butler. *The Collected Poems of W.B. Yeats.* New York: The Macmillan Company, 1965.

Index

About the Author

RAFE MARTIN is a lay Zen teacher in the Harada-Yasutani koan line. He is founding teacher of Endless Path Zendo, Rochester, New York, and was editor of Roshi Philip Kapleau's final two books. He is also an award-winning author and storyteller whose work has been cited in *Time*, *Newsweek*, the *New York Times*, and *USA Today*. His previous Buddhist books include *The Hungry Tigress, Endless Path: Awakening in the Buddhist Imagination*, and *The Banyan Deer*. He can be reached at www.endlesspathzendo.org and www.rafemartin.com.

What to Read Next
from Wisdom Publications

The Banyan Deer
A Parable of Courage & Compassion
Rafe Martin and Richard Wehrman

"*The Banyan Deer* shows that the lives of all living beings are equally important."—Ogyen Trinley Dorje, The Seventeenth Karmapa

Divine Stories
Divyāvadāna Part 1
Andy Rotman

"These stories are to the Buddhist tradition what the *Arabian Nights* is to the Arabic, an ocean of stories from which Buddhist storytellers and artists throughout Asia drew their inspiration. The translation—precise, elegant, vernacular—flows clear as water in a mountain stream."
—Wendy Doniger, Mircea Eliade Distinguished Service Professor of the History of Religions, University of Chicago

The Story of Mu
James Cordova
Illustrated by Mark Morse

"Morse's illustrations, often in warm tones, convey both the magnificence of the cosmos and the quiet grace of daily life . . . an accessible rendition of a vital Buddhist concept."—*Publishers Weekly*

About Wisdom Publications

Wisdom Publications is the leading publisher of classic and contemporary Buddhist books and practical works on mindfulness. To learn more about us or to explore our other books, please visit our website at wisdompubs.org or contact us at the address below.

Wisdom Publications
199 Elm Street
Somerville, MA 02144 USA

We are a 501(c)(3) organization, and donations in support of our mission are tax deductible.

Wisdom Publications is affiliated with the Foundation for the Preservation of the Mahayana Tradition (FPMT).